A Taste of Water

Christianity Through Taoist–Buddhist Eyes

world relig

Chwen Jiuan A. Lee

Thomas G. Hand

*2 notes in the bk so reproduce 6,
a consolation w/ our Scripture—
as they n x st do not exist—*

Paulist Press
New York ❧ *Mahwah*

Imprimi Potest
Paul F. Belcher, S.J.
Provincial, California Province of the Society of Jesus
August 2, 1989

Book design by Kathleen Doyle

Library of Congress Cataloging-in-Publication Data

Lee, Chwen Jiuan A. (Chwen Jiuan Agnes), 1941–
    A taste of water: Christianity through Taoist-Buddhist eyes/ Chwen Jiuan A. Lee, Thomas G. Hand.
      p. cm.
    Includes bibliographical references.
    ISBN 0-8091-3149-8
    1. Christianity and other religions—Taoism. 2. Christianity and other religions—Mahayana Buddhism. 3. Taoism—Relations—Christianity. 4. Mahayana Buddhism—Relations—Christianity. 5. Lee, Chwen Jiuan A. Chen Jiuan Agnes), 1941–   . 6. Hand, Thomas G., 1920–   . 7. Jesus Christ—Person and offices. 8. Spiritual life—Catholic authors. I. Hand, Thomas G., 1920–   . II. Title.
BR128.T34L44   1990
261.2'9514—dc20   90-31317
                                             CIP

Published by Paulist Press
997 Macarthur Boulevard
Mahwah, New Jersey 07430

Printed and bound in the United States of America

Contents

To the Sisters of Mercy
Burlingame, California

Thomas, one of the twelve, said to Jesus,
  "What is the kingdom of God?"
Jesus handed a cup of water to Thomas
  and said, "Here, taste this."
Thomas asked, "But—
  what is the kingdom of God?"
Jesus smiled and said nothing.
With this Thomas was filled with the Holy Spirit.

(the authors)

Preface

Begun in the west (California) this book has been completed in the east (Taiwan) over four years later. This is only fitting because it is truly a product of both east and west.

A: I was born in Taiwan and, of course, have a full Chinese name, Lee Chwen Jiuan, but I also have a western name, Sister Agnes, which I received when I entered a largely western religious community. Also, all of my university studies, right up to Ph.D., were done in the United States.

T: And I, although born and raised in California, spent the majority of my adult years, twenty-nine to be exact, in Japan. There I entered wholeheartedly into formal Zen training for six years and have continued on in Zen practice and study for fourteen years. Also, I have a Japanese name. Hand has been turned into Hando and it is written with two beautiful ideograms meaning "to accompany (others) in crossing over."

These points are important because our book is largely autobiographical. This applies not only to the many little episodes from our personal experiences that are interspersed throughout these pages, but even more to the whole book, because both of us have experienced the vivifying light eastern philosophies of life and eastern practices can shed on Jesus Christ and his teaching. To be specific, it is the study and practice of Mahayana Buddhism and classical Taoism, more than any other element in our spiritual quest, that have assisted us to become better Christians.

Both singly and sometimes together, we have pre-

1

sented many of the ideas written here to various audiences over a period of five to ten years. Encouraged by their response and urged by our own experience, we have collaborated on this book. The subjects taken up we see as crucial and all important for the evolutionary advance of human consciousness. We can only hope that we have not darkened matters. There is a Chinese tradition that a person should not write anything before the age of forty. We both amply qualify on this count, but the enlightenment expected to accompany such age is another matter. At least we have the maturity to know that what we present in these pages is not any kind of definitive statement. Rather it is a sincere, exploratory examination into what the east might tell us about Jesus Christ and his fundamental teachings.

We want to be very clear about what we have attempted to do. From our own study and experience we have tried to look at Jesus of Nazareth and the Christian path through Taoist/Buddhist eyes. Also, during the years of writing, ideas on the evolution of consciousness were seen to mesh so perfectly with the whole thrust of the book that we have employed them to strengthen our presentation. These ideas on the course of human evolution have been especially illuminating in regard to the life of Jesus and his advancement to the highest spirit consciousness through his death and in his resurrection.

One point to be emphasized is that we realize perfectly well that some of our formulations about God, Jesus and human life do differ from conventional Christian teaching, including that of the Catholic Church. We have consistently presented these interpretations not as our fixed positions, but as what we feel the great Taoist and Buddhist masters might say from their enlightened viewpoint. We offer them not as dogmas, but only as options as to how the original Christian teachings may well be interpreted and

As Paul lived a Jewish grid to his perception of reve-
so then bh. bugs an Eastern" grid.

Preface 3

understood under the impact of contact with the light of
eastern philosophies of life. Both of us, as Catholics, are
quite happy to ultimately follow the directives of the
church community.

Both of us have made our lifelong option to follow the
footsteps of Jesus, the Christ and are enjoying our fellow-
ship as members of his faith community. We are firmly
convinced that any religious doctrine is only a finger
pointing to the moon, subject to new understanding as
religious experience matures and deepens. Over the more
than ten years of our quest in inculturation, inter-religious
dialogue and inter-faith experience, both of us have sometimes been challenged, even with an air of disapproval:
"But one has to be faithful to one's own tradition." Hearing this kind of uneasy cry, we've often questioned ourselves, "Is there such a thing as a fixed, unchanging tradition or culture or religious consciousness? What does it
really mean to be faithful and loyal to tradition?" These
questions force us to turn to inner experience as the
only foundation for advancement and expansion of consciousness.

Fortunately, the church does allow for a development
of dogma and for a certain plurality of expressions. In a
speech in January 1988, Cardinal Willebrands, president
of the Secretariat for Promoting Christian Unity, stated
that a major Catholic-Orthodox advance came in a 1982
dialogue session which produced "acceptance of unity of
faith within a possible diversity of formulas and expressions."[1] We see no reason why this diversity within the
church cannot also be born from the dialogue with the
other great spiritual paths of humanity.

As an example of how eastern thought and practice
can bring new light to the Christian mysteries and even
correct some rather dark areas, we would like to recom-

mend the works of the great Benedictine monk, Swami Abhishiktananda. He has already superbly done from the Hindu (especially Vedantist Advaita) viewpoint, what we are here attempting from the Taoist/Buddhist. For instance, speaking about the Christian theological dispute about grace and free will, he says:

> Both parties were in fact victims of the same dualistic prejudice which seeks to add together God and man. Advaita means precisely this: neither God alone, nor creature alone, nor God plus creature, but an indefinable non-duality which transcends at once all separation and confusion.[2]

Later, he points out the ultimate Hindu-Christian unity:

> In reality the Advaita lies at the root of Christian experience. It is simply the mystery *that God and the world are not two.*[3]

We sincerely feel that none of the major spiritual paths are a threat to the Christian church. Rather, they present a challenge to accept their light, for it can wonderfully help all to know what human life is and also to understand more deeply Jesus Christ, the human archetype personified. At the same time we can all be inspired to walk more boldly and faithfully the path to spirit consciousness.

A: Chwen Jiuan A. Lee, SMIC
Sheng Kung Sisters
House of Formation
Tahsi, Taiwan,
R.O.C.

T: Thomas G. Hand, S.J.
Mercy Center
Burlingame,
California, U.S.A.

Authors' Note

In writing this book we have constantly been faced with the question of which words to capitalize. The problem arises because that very principle which underlies all the changing phenomena of life is humanly felt to be mysterious, infinite, divine. Its experience calls forth reverence and even awe. This feeling is often expressed in English by capitalizing all terms referring to this principle. But our references are so numerous and all pervasive that we have chosen to restrict capitalization only to such terms as God and Trinity, where a lack of capitals might lead to confusion and perhaps consternation.

Capitalize all life

1. *God Is Different*

God is the groundless Ground   *eternal ?*
with neither size nor limit.
He who is aware of this
has the awakened Spirit.

—*Angelus Silesius*[1]

T: About twenty-five years ago when I was staying at a retreat house in Tokyo, a young Japanese lady came for a talk. She had recently left the training program of a religious community and wanted some help in determining her future path. As we talked I mentioned that in Japan we always talk about the Way of Tea (*Sado*), the Way of Flowers (*Kado*), the Soft Way (*Judo*) of self-defense, and so forth; but there is no word of where all these paths are going. We speak of the Way *of,* but never the Way *to.* So, I asked her where these paths lead to. She was totally nonplussed and couldn't answer anything. I then somewhat smugly pointed out that every path is a way to God.

It all seemed so clear to my western mind. However, I can remember that even at that time, I felt that this all too familiar statement was somehow off the mark. Certainly I knew that I was being very western. Now after years of thought and dialogue I know that as a western voice I seemed to have said something enlightening, but by being too categorical I actually confused the issue—that her eastern voice seemed to have said nothing and yet somehow clarified the whole question. Let us begin, then, by considering how the east approaches the mystery we call God.

7

Who/What Is God?

The west seems to be far more concerned with ideas about God than the east is. Is there a God? What is God like? How is God personal? If God is good how can he allow all this evil? These are questions that echo all down the ages of western history. The Christian answer is that there is only one supreme, infinite, personal being, who creates and rules everything. The Christian creed begins, "We believe in one God, the Father, the Almighty, maker of heaven and earth, of all that is seen and unseen." To such a mentality the existence of other entire cultures in which the concept of a supreme, infinite, personal creator is hardly dealt with at all is practically inconceivable. When Francis Xavier gave the first Christian sermons in Japan as late as the sixteenth century, he could find no suitable word for God and the early missionaries finally had to settle for the Latin word *Deus.* When Catholic missionaries returned to Japan in the late nineteenth century, they ended up using the word the Catholics had created in China, *Tenshu,* Lord of heaven. Finally, in recent years in Japan, the indigenous term *Kami* is used, but originally it by no means expressed the meaning Christians have come to give it.

What does this tell us about the Chinese and Japanese? The old western answer to such a question was that they are all "benighted pagans" who need to listen to the revelation of the personal God given in the Christian gospel. Happily, such Christian pride and narrowness is gradually dissipating under the increasing impact of the lives and teachings of many, many enlightened easterners. It is perfectly clear that these "non-Christians" have experienced what we call God and that their teachings certainly manifest the presence of the Holy Spirit. But the westerner is still left with the enigma of cultures without a "supreme God." Again, what are we to make of this?

Noble Silence

Buddha himself gives us the basic answer. India, as the midpoint between east and west, has a superabundance of superb concepts and teachings about the nature of God. However, around 500 B.C., when the great enlightened one (Buddha) began to communicate his experience to others, these teachings had atrophied into a religion which demanded blind acceptance of the Vedas as infallible dogma. Shakyamuni Buddha, on the other hand, was only interested in helping people to the experience of God. Thus it is said that whenever he was asked about God and the divine nature, he simply maintained a "noble silence." He taught the path and after that—silence. We find this same reluctance to speak about a personal ultimate throughout the far east even today. Of course, there is an immense number of "gods." The myriad of *kami* in Japan and the innumerable *shen* and *gon* in China are still reverenced. But none of these even approaches the clearly defined, infinite deity of Christian theology.

Certainly we can say that the east prefers not to conceptualize the absolute. It is true that Sino-Japanese Shingon Buddhism has received a wealth of conceptual doctrine from India. In Japanese Shingon Buddhism, for example, there is a marvelously elaborated cosmic system with *Dai Nichi* (lit. *Dai* = great, *Nichi* = sun) at the summit. However, no scholar would equate *Dai Nichi* with the God of Christianity. The whole frame of reference of Shingon Buddhism and Christianity is too different. Also, an easterner is by no means as attached to doctrinal systems as, say, a Christian is to the Nicene Creed. There are no eternal dogmas that must be preserved against all heretical opponents. From an eastern point of view the glorification of theology in the west is a great and serious obstacle to seeing. For an easterner a conceptual framework is only a tool to be used on the path to that knowing which is beyond all concepts. This expedient use of concepts is an example of the Indian advice to use a thorn to take out a thorn. Use dogma to go beyond dogma. And since dogmas are only a means to the end, no one set of dogmas is uniquely and exclusively correct and salvific. As the Chinese say, *san chiao kuei i,* "The three teachings—Buddhism, Confucianism and Taoism—return to one."

Thus the east tells us that if dogmas are used without fear or attachment, they can truly help us along the path and assist us in teaching the path to others, but all must eventually fade in the light of transconceptual reality. It is for this reason that our Zen master, Yamada Koun Roshi, taught us that words with meaning are dead, but words of no meaning are alive. This is because words with meaning narrow us to their frame of reference, whereas words without meaning both frustrate our ordinary categorical consciousness and provide a kind of vehicle for the contemplative movement of a human being toward the enlightened state of seeing what is.

Here we can now note how often and how fittingly paradox is used to express and to bring us to the world of enlightenment. This is especially true of the eastern way of teaching. In a paradox, words are used, but not according to the pattern of ordinary reason. Thus mental activity is totally frustrated, and, as it drops away, direct knowing can arise. The modern Japanese Zen Master Suzuki Shunryu Roshi is quoted as saying, "There is no God. But he is always with you." A particularly appropriate paradox for the Americans Suzuki Roshi was speaking to. The east would certainly agree with the cry of St. Gregory Nazianzen, "By what name shall I call you who are beyond all names?"

God Is Different

T: I was walking one September morning on the roof of our language school in Kamakura, Japan. I had already started my formal Zen training and certainly the whole Zen world, which was still so full of enigmas to me, had begun its powerful impact on my consciousness. I wasn't thinking about anything special and was just gazing at a not particularly beautiful cloud bank over in the west, when I suddenly realized that *God is different*. It wasn't anything like a blinding flash of enlightenment. Just a shift of consciousness in which I understood that God is different from all that I had been taught or thought about "him." It has taken years of struggle to accept, elucidate and develop the insight of that morning. At the time all I did was keep repeating to myself throughout the day, "God is different, God is different!"

The first point that became clear to me was that we must never put God into a numbered series or into opposition to the multitude of individual beings. Even from my teens I had puzzled over the problem of how to love God and creatures. We were taught that we should love God *first*. Creatures were always to come second in the love of our wills even though our affections might not be able to follow such an order. Religious life was presented as a style of life in which God had chosen one as his special beloved and one should not give one's heart to any creature. On the other hand, such a human devotion was considered acceptable for married people. In this whole conceptual system God is put somehow into opposition to and even into competition with creatures. In this frame of reference we make clear distinctions between creatures and God, human and divine, nature and grace. We look upon ourselves as distinct from but in relationship to God, who is the other to all creatures. The spiritual path is usually conceived of as striving to come to the perfect relationship of love for God. *in west of*

However, when we conceive of an *actual* distinction and relationship between God and creatures, we are in effect putting God into a *category* separate from the creature category. To separate the formless and forms (its manifestations) into two is to place the formless into a category. True, God's category is called "infinite" and "absolute," but nonetheless it is category. We have given boundaries to the boundless. The east would say that such a conception of God is a product of relational experience. That it does not spring from the ultimate experience of the actual God. The real God is different from all such categorization. In the final experience of God there is no question of separation, distinction or relationship. The distinguishing intellect is useless and gives way to that intuitive seeing which is best described as being. Since this experience of God is the cardinal point of the whole eastern view, we will be returning to it again and again. For now all we wish to do is to insist that God is seen as different from all western categories and to point out that in the western spiritual traditions, especially in their popular form, there is a strong tendency to conceptualize God. These concepts become dogmas and take on paramount importance. It is the opinion of most eastern masters that this conceptualizing, dogmatizing tendency, although somewhat helpful, is actually dangerous and can easily create real obstacles to

we then set up worship of our dogmas & concepts—an idolatry. as Jesus their septan that killed ✗

the experience of God. In fact, they recommend much
more of the noble silence of Shakyamuni Buddha.

Eastern God-Talk

As has already been admitted, the east does verbalize
the hierarchy of being, including the ultimate. For example
the *I Ching* (The Book of Change), the world's oldest book,
speaks of *wu chi*. *Chi* means limit, *wu* is the negative. Thus
the meaning is the limitless, the infinite. From *wu chi*
emerges *t'ai chi*, the beginning of limit. *Wu chi* takes on
form in *t'ai chi*. *T'ai chi* is the manifestation of *wu chi*.
Thus there are two fundamental principles underlying all
reality. One is infinite and formless, the other limited
form. Form is always emerging from and then returning to
the formless, *wu chi*. It is this movement that accounts for
our whole constantly changing world.

Here we must add an important point. There are no
temples, no devotions to *wu chi* as such. There is devotion
to thousands of its manifestations, but this ultimate is
never conceived of as an other, as a person, to whom devotion and worship are offered. The east does not deny
God. Nor is it unconscious of the absolute. Rather, it has
vigorously maintained what the west calls both the transcendence and immanence of the ultimate. Transcendence
because it refuses to get caught up in dogmatic categorization of God. Immanence because it maintains a high level
of sense of the mystery as present in all beings and events.
As the Chinese say, *wu chi* permeates "the four directions
and eight corners."

As is obvious, in such a consciousness there is no room
for a personal God in the fashion of the west. In western
traditions the ultimate God is the person, the other to
whom we offer worship and devotion. Of course there are

innumerable devotions in eastern religions. *Namu Amida
Bu* (*tsu*) (I entrust myself to Amida Buddha) is the basic
mantra of Pure Land Buddhism and the billions of daily
recitations of *Namu Amida Bu* (*tsu*) in Japanese and *Namo
Amito Fu* in Chinese are ample testimony to the devotional
heart of the east. But even the devotees of Amida Buddha
would not claim for Amida the highly personal relatedness
of the Christian God. The whole thing is left open and
mysterious. Again we must conclude that the Far East does
not describe God like the west does.

A: In the early years of my Christian experience I
felt very uneasy about Christian God-talk. For example, so
often in the course of a retreat I would sit there during the
director's talk wondering to myself, "Does he really *know*
what he is talking about?" I wrote time and time again in
my retreat notes, *ch'iang tsu to li* (forced words steal life
away). For more than ten years after my baptism into the
Christian faith at the age of seventeen, I listened to many
sermons and talks, but I must honestly say that very little
of the God-talk really resonated within me. I kept saying to
myself that the God whom I can understand with my limited mind is not worthy of my bended knees.

One day in 1969, a Chinese priest spoke to us about
Mary, the mother of Jesus, and for the first time there was
something that clicked. His words carried life. I even wrote
two lines in celebration and showed them to the sister
sitting next to me: "This theologian is such a genius, he
even makes sense out of mystery!" However, to this I must
add that I feel not only much more comfortable these days,
but even excited about the Christian opening to the east.
Everywhere we see eastern Christians struggling to give
birth to a genuine spirituality that is both Christian and
indigenous (in my case, Chinese). I was so happy when we

hung up a scroll of Chinese calligraphy with the first two
lines taken from the first chapter of Lao Tzu: *Tao Te Ching*
at the entrance of our chapel in Tainan, Taiwan.

Chinese God-Talk

A: One day in the course of a discussion Father
Hand said to me, "Give me an example of Chinese God-
talk." Without even thinking I answered, "There is none.
We don't have it, simply because in our consciousness we
don't have such a segregation between God and human
beings." However, when he insisted, I suggested this very
chapter of *Tao Te Ching*.

> The *tao* (way) that can be expressed
>   is not the unchanging *tao*.
> The name that can be named
>   is not the unchanging name.
> "*Wu*" (formless) names the origin of heaven
>   and earth.
> "*Yu*" (form) names the mother of the ten
>   thousand things.
> Therefore, stay in *wu,* if you desire to penetrate
>   the mystery;
> Stay in *yu,* if you desire to penetrate the
>   manifestation.
> These two (*wu* and *yu*) have the same origin,
>   but are different names.
> Both are mystery, mystery upon mystery, the
>   door of all wonders.[2]

These lines are the best translation we have been able
to work out for the fifty-nine Chinese ideograms which
constitute the first chapter of the *Tao Te Ching*. This clas-

sic text is attributed to Lao Tzu and is variously dated from
the fourth to sixth century B.C. It is interesting to note that
it was written about the same time that Shakyamuni
Buddha arrived at his enlightenment in India.

In order to present at least something of the richness
and enlightening depth of this passage in contemporary
language, we will not make a detailed commentary but
simply offer a free and somewhat expanded paraphrase.

> The life flow that can be expressed in concepts
>> and words
>> is not the eternal, unchanging life flow.
> The designation of this life flow that is actually
>> a categorizing name
>> does not really name the eternal, unchanging.
> As the reality underlying the whole phenomenal
>> world,
>> it is beyond all designation, formless.
> As the reality that is actually manifesting in the
>> myriad of forms in the phenomenal world,
>> it can be named with a myriad of names.
> Therefore, have a contemplative heart totally
>> detached
>> from all categories in order to see the mystery.
> Have a heart that fully enters into the world of
>> forms
>> in order to truly see the mystery in the
>> manifestations.
> Although these two, the unmanifest and the
>> manifestations,
>> have been designated by different names,
>> they are actually one and the same reality.
> Inasmuch as they are the same reality, they are
>> dark.

> Darkness of darkness!
> —The gate to all mystery!

Because the experiential identity of the formless and all forms is beyond all conceptual knowledge, Lao Tzu calls it dark, unknowable and in so many words exhorts us to enter into this ultimate darkness so that we can *see* the mystery of life. This chapter of Lao Tzu, in spite of, or perhaps because of, its antiquity, is one of the most sophisticated examples of "God-talk" in all classical Chinese literature, but even so, it is nothing like the elaborate theological treatises or even the creeds of the west. Any serious meditation upon it will reveal that it springs from experiential knowing and that in this experience the distinctions we make with our ordinary consciousness are not actually present in the author's awareness. Because of this it is not, strictly speaking, theology. *Tao Te Ching* is a record of mystical experience. The frame of reference and the level of awareness that it expresses is not that of our usual state. Let us therefore examine this level of awareness more closely, in particular, the loss of self that it requires.

2. *I Am Different*

> In the depth
>> of the autumn sky
> I found—
>> myself.

> *—Seisei*

A: About fifteen years ago while teaching at our community's high school in Taiwan, I had a rather difficult but very special student who often surprised me with unexpected questions about life and the human situation. One afternoon when all the students were outside cleaning up the campus, she came running up to me and said, "Sister Lee, tell me, when is the time that you are the happiest?" At that moment I had no response for her, because I had not really observed myself and my emotions. So I answered, "Give me a couple of days to observe myself and then I will give you an answer." During the next two days I discovered existentially that I am most happy when I am not thinking of myself. When there is no return to self, I have no anxiety about the past, no present worry, no anticipation about the future. I am simply in the very flow of life. This is when I really enjoy life.

This little story presents the two points we wish to take up next as we develop the possible influence of eastern insights on modern Christian spirituality: the human concern for self and the loss of this self. In the first chapter we merely introduced a few eastern insights about God. Before going further into this investigation it will be helpful to consider both the self and the loss of self as essential elements of the human path. This question of self and its

19

loss must be faced squarely and boldly because to most westerners the experiential loss of self is almost inconceivable. Nowadays especially, the pendulum has swung far over to the side of self-discovery, self-improvement, self-expression and self-determination. We certainly do admit that there is a place for such ego development. However, on the other hand, in this age when everyone is encouraged to "do it my way," to talk of losing self may seem totally out of date. Nevertheless, the call of eastern (and western) masters is radical and insistent: without the loss of self there can be no discovery of the true self.

Separate Self

What, then, is the human self? How does it obstruct our happiness? In what sense must it be actually let go of as false and illusory? What is the true self and how do we come to know it? The east teaches insistently that our ordinary way of identifying ourselves is a "mis-take." We take ourselves for something we are not. Without going into the difficult question of how and why this mistake is made, the fact is that we ordinarily identify ourselves as *separate* individuals in a world made up of a huge multiplicity of beings. We do hear about the oneness of everything, and sometimes a vague sense of the communion of all beings breaks in on our awareness, but for most of us full expansion of consciousness in which separation is lost is rare or almost never experienced.

Our consistent self-identification is "*I* am simply not *you*. I am not *he, she, this* or *that*." We are related in some way, but the individual *I* and the individual *you, this* and *that* always make up nothing more than a plural number. Our skin line is a wall of separation. In fact it is precisely this persistent identification of our selves with our bodies that is largely at the root of our separated egos. Freud has rightly pointed out that our egos are mainly "body egos." It is not the consciousness of ourselves as *individuals,* but the consistent apprehension of ourselves as *separate* individuals that is mistaken. This may sound like a strange statement, but admittedly we are dealing here with the very mystery of our human being, and ultimately this cannot be truly expressed in our dualistic language. However, at this stage of our investigation this way of expressing it is adequate.

We instinctively try to bridge this gap of separation between self and others by various kinds of relationship, but without enlightenment the impression remains that the only awareness we can have of ourselves is that of my self irrevocably separate from your self. With this kind of self-identification comes an immense drive for self-preservation, self-defense and self-development. We can hardly fault such drives. But because of our ordinary egocentric consciousness, we fear and worry about any other person or thing that threatens the well-being of this self. We are attracted to and attach ourselves to whatever can assure self-survival and increase self-importance. The whole inner world of fear, worry, anticipation, attachment, tension stress, even breakdown or total withdrawal arises out of this awareness of self as a separate, threatened individual.

The same process takes place on the social level as humans group themselves into "separate" tribes, nations, religions and other social units. Aggressive or defensive nationalism, chauvinism, tension, confrontation, cold wars and hot wars all arise from the same kind of consciousness that divides individuals.

T: Yasutani Hakuun Roshi was a great Japanese Zen master. When I made my first and only *sesshin* retreat under his direction, he was over eighty years of age, a man of profound vitality and strength. This was obviously the strength of true inner experience. I can still see him, a rather small, quite thin person with a strong jaw and big ears. I especially remember him glowing with conviction as he gave his *teisho* (formal talks sharing enlightened awareness). One thing he often repeated was the need to radically let go of all judgment, all categorical thinking, and become like a white sheet of paper. Fittingly, his Zen name, Hakuun, meant White Cloud. In this context he not only glowed but almost glowered at us, stressing the need to let go of the personal self (*ji ga*). But this was not enough. One must let go of the family self (*ie no ga*) and the national self (*kuni no ga*) and especially the religious self (*shukyo no ga*). Each family, nation and religion is a kind of individual reality. Being a part of these realities constitutes much of our self-identity. Hakuun Roshi insisted that we must lose all these selves if we are to come to enlightenment. In fact, Zen is primarily concerned with what we can call the self/ Self. We are to forget the self, come to the Self and ultimately to the self/Self. This approach can be contrasted with western spirituality, which focuses much more on finding not self, but God. But, as we shall see, it comes to the very same process.

The self/Self

The successor to Hakuun Roshi was Yamada Koun Roshi. Not long after I became his disciple I was given as my practice to go deeper and deeper into the question, "Who is the one hearing?" Actually, the question was given in Japanese, "*Kikunushi, nani mono zo?*" which literally

means, "The master hearing, what kind of being, really?"
Kiku means hearing. *Nushi* is master, lord, owner, the one
who bears all the responsibility. The question, then, is not
simply "Who (What) am I?" which could get rather abstract. Rather it is a matter of going into this present act of
hearing. Who is hearing this airplane right now? Who is the
one that can say that this act of hearing is *my* action? What
is this "owner" like? The whole Buddhist path is well expressed by the thirteenth century master, Dogen, founder
of the Soto Zen path in Japan.

> To learn the path (of Buddha) is to learn the self.
> To learn the self is to forget self.
> To forget self is to perceive self as all things.
>
> —*Shobogenzo, Genjokoan*
> (Our translation)

The other main Zen path in Japan is Rinzai. The
founder of this line, the ninth century Chinese master Lin
Chi (*Rinzai* in Japanese), also constantly urged his monks
to look for the Self. He says:

> Over this mass of reddish flesh there is one true
> person
>   of no rank.
> This one is coming in and out of your sense
> organs
>   all the time.
> If you have not yet witnessed (to) this fact,
>   Look! Look!
>
> —*Rinzairoku*
> (Our translation)

It is this "true person of no rank" that all of Zen is focused upon.

Another famous Zen question is, "What is your face before your parents were born?" This puzzling *koan* (a pithy expression of enlightenment) actually contains its answer in the very question itself and brings us to the next step in our investigation into the self. If I have a face before my parents were born, it can only mean that "I" am a reality that is somehow outside the temporal framework in which, of course, I usually identify myself. This "I" is outside the category of time. It is eternal. Note here that the word eternal means not only without end but also without beginning. Time categories simply do not apply. Lin Chi's "true person of no rank" is even more explicit. "Of no rank" means totally outside all categories of time, space, sense, imagination or intellect. The self that Dogen calls upon us to forget is, again, this categorical self such as male or female, old or young, Mexican or Canadian, etc. Only the awareness that has lost this self can "perceive self as all things"! It is precisely because we are all ultimately this one Self that we are not actually separate. The categorical self that we so treasure and guard is nothing but an individual manifestation of the one being. As long as the individual is all that we are aware of, we are bound to fall into the mis-take of separatism with all its sad consequences. Finding the boundless Self brings all into balance and only then is even the truth of our individuality known.

The Middle Way

In all this we are following the teaching of Mahayana Buddhism, which is known as the middle way. It teaches that one should deny neither the relational multiplicity of

individual beings before our eyes nor the absolute unity of
all. The one and the many are both true. This is clearly
expressed in the famous lines from the *Heart Sutra,* a short
sutra that is constantly recited by millions of Buddhists.

> Form is not different from emptiness;
> Emptiness is not different from form.
> Form, this is emptiness;
> Emptiness, this is form.

> (Our translation)

Form, of course, refers to *all* categorical beings (literally,
the word is "color" in the text). Emptiness is the non-categorical reality which is manifested in all forms. In fact,
"form" could be made plural in the English translation of
the Chinese, which itself is both singular and plural:
"Forms are not different from emptiness," and vice versa.
These short verses are an attempt to take us beyond the
restrictions of our differentiating language.

Language, as we almost invariably use it, is categorical. So how can we express in words the eternal, non-categorical "true person of no rank"? We must be extremely
careful as we write, and you must be the same as you read
anything written about the "one Self." *We must not make
"it" into just another category.* Our minds are doing this
unless they are truly enlightened. As we shall see in the next
chapter, it is only our heart that knows without categorizing. If the one Self is just an "other" category, then it is
distinct from the phenomenal self and our separation is
only compounded. The Self is not some thing or some one
that is in opposition to our self. Each one of us is simply
self/Self. Strictly speaking, when talking about the one Self

and the phenomenal self, one cannot say both or they. The one word "I" can say the truth, but only when this is the "I" of an enlightened person. As you can see, the only thing to do is to return to the level of experience that is beneath our ordinary differentiating perception of things.

Actualization of the Middle Way

Before investigating further the kind of awareness in which we know the Self, it will be helpful to hear from a few people who have had this experience. It is upon such experiences as these that the whole teaching about the loss of self is based. The following examples have been chosen because they are experiences of ordinary people of our day and age. All are westerners who were following the Zen path under a Japanese master. These experiences are called *kensho,* a Japanese term which means "seeing (one's) nature" and refers to the first glimpse of the one Self. Only great and definitive breakthroughs are spoken of as *satori.* The accounts are from *Kyosho,* the magazine of the Zen group to which both of us belonged in Japan.

From *Kensho Account,* by C.:

> That moment (the moment of realizing one's essential nature) came five days after the close of sesshin—a very ordinary moment in my daily routine. I was in the classroom at the Ateneo de Manila University, waiting for my students to finish a written examination. From where I stood, I could look out at the campus—at a huge acacia tree swaying in the gentle breeze. As the time passed, I stood watching the swaying branch of

the tree. Suddenly, there was nothing. Nothing but the swaying tree: no I watching, just I the swaying branch, weightless in the breeze, empty and light: no thoughts, just free, just This!

... Afterwards, as I walked across the campus, the peace and tranquility welling up in me seemed to emanate from every flower and leaf along the walk, from the cluster of pigeons ... from the dazzling sun ... from the old caretaker ... I was One with every pulsing sign of life.[1]

In *My Experience of Kensho,* S. writes:

Everything was melting together and I was melting into everything just as a piece of ice melts into water. I was no longer afraid for there was nothing to fear. There was no difference between life and death. I was happy for the first time in my life and so very grateful.

... There was no such thing as loneliness.

I know that I had always judged things in relation to myself, because I was a separate entity.

Finally, in *My Way to Enlightenment,* L. expresses her experience very clearly:

One afternoon, as I was looking out of the window into the crown of an ancient tree, my thoughts, with great intensity, spiralled from reflections upon my own life ever deeper into the Nature of Dharma (here the Buddhist term Dharma means simply, Reality). And as my "self" was melting away into something infinitely larger than myself,

there was just one huge wave of warmth, Love and
Delight. At last, there was only One, not two.
There is nothing but the Dharma. Nothing else. I
am myself: just this.

Later the question of my identity arose and I
realized with great clarity and Joy that as a person
*I am the Dharma as it manifests itself in the way of
L.* This is my *true nature.* It does not belong to me.
(Nothing that belongs; no-one to whom it belongs). It is the ever-changing *right-here-now. L.*'s
way can never be separate from the actuality *of
this moment.* It has no form. It cannot be pinned
down, for it has no substance. But *it is.* This is like
trying to explain a waterfall by taking one drop
and trying to demonstrate the meaning of a waterfall. But meanwhile the waterfall is just *water
falling thus,* that's all.

Then, later on, during a walk outside:

Everything shone forth with incredible simplicity of Being, of which I was an integral part. It
is really impossible to describe, for actually there
was no "I" who was experiencing or thinking this.
Just utter, utter, utter peaceful thusness. Nothing
special!

In all countries and ages and in all religions it is easy to
find accounts of experiences such as these. The examples
are innumerable. The conceptual frame of reference in
which the event is related will vary, of course, but the
ineffable experience itself is fundamentally the same, precisely because it is beyond all categories. And always essential to the experience is the loss of the ordinary self-
identification.

"no I watching . . . just This!"–(C)

"It is really impossible to describe, for actually, there was no 'I' who was experiencing or thinking this."–(L)

The main point here is that in this state of awareness, although the person remains an individual, she/he is *no longer experienced as ultimately separate!* You are an individual. The book you are now reading is also an individual being. You, the book, and every thing are all individual manifestations of the same reality. There are no you and I and this book all as separate beings, but only *one,* non-categorical being existing in an infinite variety of categorical manifestations. L. expresses this very well: ". . . as a person *I am the Dharma* (Reality) *as it manifests itself in the way of L.* This is my *true nature.* It does not belong to me. (Nothing that belongs; no-one to whom it belongs)."

The *kensho* experiences given above not only manifest for us the self/Self of true knowledge, but also exemplify the characteristics of that shift in consciousness we call enlightenment. Both as an introduction to a further investigation into this consciousness and as a conclusion to this section on self, we can compare short poems from two famous poets, one of the west, the other of the east.

Alfred Lord Tennyson writes:

Flower in the crannied wall,
I pluck you out of the crannies,
I hold you here, root and all, in my hand,
Little flower—*if* I could understand
What you are, root and all, and all in all,
I should know what God and man is.

Clearly Tennyson is touching on our ultimate concern here, to "know what God and man is." He is right in seeking it in the concrete reality, say, of a little flower. Also, he is very insightful to make the last verb *is,* not "what God and man *are.*" But in this quest he has taken the route of speculation, diagnosis and analysis. He has to pluck out the flower, root and all, to analyze it, as it were. And there is no certainty in his knowledge even though he holds it in his hand. The flower and he are still separated and all is *if* and *could* and *should.*

On the other hand, the seventeenth century Japanese poet Matsuo Basho describes his experience of plum flowers in a different way:

With the scent of plum blossoms	Ume ga ka ni
Suddenly the sun rises—	Notto hi no deru—
The mountain path.	Yamaji kana.

In this *haiku* (poem) Basho is presenting his direct experience of plum blossoms, sunrise and mountain path. He is not *thinking about* these things. He is simply experiencing them. There is no "I" or "my" in his awareness. Without this subjective return to self, he feels the oneness of everything in the scene. The sun rises *with* the scent of blossoms. The scent, the sun, the path and Basho himself are just one flow. Because this formless flow is identical with every form, such as a flower, sun, path and Basho, the experience, while happening within a few minutes two centuries ago, is nonetheless universal. When we meet this experience in Basho's *haiku,* something resonates within us and our awareness is easily turned toward his enlightened state of awareness. We are drawn toward natural, direct, enlightened knowing.

3. *When the Light Turns On*

The clearer I perceive
that which is True,
the less reasoning, judging, arguing
I can do.

—Angelus Silesius

T: About twenty-two years ago I was standing on the platform of the old Seki Machi train station in a very quiet section of Tokyo. I was looking at the tracks, not thinking of anything in particular, when suddenly there was a kind of shift in my consciousness. It was a very small experience, but I still remember it as somehow significant. At the time I classified it as a peek into the "interior world." I often used to describe myself as a case of arrested consciousness. I don't know exactly what this meant, but at that train station I knew that a whole new world had opened out to my consciousness for a moment. I felt quietly excited and happy as I walked up and down on the platform awaiting the train. I believe now that it was actually a tiny glance at the world which is neither interior nor exterior, but just *is*. Let us, then, consider the *kind of awareness* that reveals that which is. Following the tradition of the east we begin with an example, not a tiny experience like mine, but of a true enlightenment. We go back to eighteenth century Japan.

It was very early in the morning at a Zen monastery near the town of Takeda, northwest across the mountains from Edo (Tokyo). The monks were close to the end of a strict retreat. The man who was to become one of the greatest of all Japanese Zen masters, Hakuin, was seated in

31

profound meditation in a small temple some distance from
the main hall. The deep sound of the temple bell calling all
to the chanting of the sutras broke the morning stillness.
Upon hearing the sound Hakuin was enlightened and
shouted out with joy, "I just rang!" Now, of course, Hakuin
knows that he is he and the bell is the bell. But he truly
means it when he says, "*I* just rang!" His knowledge in this
experience is clearly different from our usual awareness.

The Light Turns On

As pointed out in the last chapter, in order to truly
know reality, we must come to a different kind of knowing
than the ordinary categorical knowledge by which we know
ourselves and all else. The experience of this new knowledge as it arises within a person is called enlightenment.
Again we must insist that this knowledge is not, strictly
speaking, of a "different kind" in the sense that one can
speak of sense knowledge and mental knowledge as being
different one to the other. Enlightenment is not to be lined
up in a series with other kinds of awareness, just as God is
not to be put into a series with "other" beings. Enlightenment is not in the realm of categories, not just *another,*
albeit higher, kind of knowing. It is direct reality experience and it arises within the very activities of the senses
and imagination and intellect. In this regard, the word
enlightenment itself is most interesting. It is as if a light
turns on and within the activity of our ordinary powers of
knowledge the non-exclusiveness, the boundlessness of reality is revealed.
It is extremely difficult to write about true knowing.
However, because our very salvation depends upon this
awakening, we must do our best to describe it with the

limiting, categorical words at our disposal. As we shall see, these words, too, when used in a non-exclusive way by an enlightened mind, can be the occasion for a person's entry into the light of life.

The Light of Reality

The essential characteristic of such knowledge is that it is *direct* experience. In it the human mind does not abstract an idea and know the object through this idea. In fact, that which is known is not seen as an object at all. The self does not stand back and know something as an object. Rather, the knower, the act of knowing, and that which is known are all one. Take for example the experience expressed in the sentence, "I am looking at a tree." Clearly this expression indicates a subject, "I," looking at an object, "tree." As I get to know categorically more about the tree, I can say, "I am looking at a redwood tree." Since there are dawn redwoods native to China, I must further qualify the tree by saying, "I am looking at a California redwood tree." We can continue along this line of knowing and classify the tree as a "young, healthy, on my neighbor's property, beautiful, small, etc., California redwood tree." This is all categorical knowledge. That is why we say "a" tree, i.e., one being in the tree category.

However, within this differentiating knowledge itself another experience is present, even though most of the time we are not aware of it. The tree is not just *a . . .* redwood tree, but it is *this* tree. It is within the experience of this living, here and now, redwood tree that the light can turn on and reality itself can be known. In such knowledge there are no categories or classifications. It is nothing but the naked experience of being, of reality. So naked is it that the very categories "I" (subject) and "tree" (object) and "looking at" (activity) are lost. The self is lost and all *relationship* to other persons and things also goes. "I," "tree," "looking at" are all simply being. All are one. This is why Hakuin could truly cry out, "I just rang!" My reality, my looking at and the tree's reality are experienced as one even within the experience of my looking at it as "a young, healthy . . . redwood tree."

Having come so far, we are in a position to contrast enlightenment with what we have been calling ordinary knowledge. The latter is reflexive, while enlightenment is direct. Ordinary knowledge is so reflexive that even in the statement, "I am looking at a tree," the subject "I" is actually an *object* of one's consciousness. I am conscious that *I* am seeing the tree. In this process there is always a stepping back from the actual experience and a conscious reflection on it. There is always a separation, even from one's self! As long as this knowledge is not enlightened by the concomitant experience of reality itself, as long as this is the only knowledge we experience, we are still in the throes of an agony of separation.

Because reflexive consciousness is based on a standing back from direct experience, we are able to classify, categorize, and make comparisons and judgments with it. For example, I stand back from my seeing both this tree and that tree, and I can then see that they are the same. They both belong to a class of trees, the category of oak, for example. I can compare and judge them as the same or different. With this kind of reflection I can set up standards and judge things as good or bad, beautiful or ugly, etc. In pure, direct awareness there is no standing back, no comparison, no judgment, no separation from the one flow of being.

A: The first time I was directly challenged to manifest this pure non-reflexive awareness was in an encounter with Father Shigeta Oshida, a Japanese Dominican priest. In 1978 he came to Taiwan to give our community a one week retreat. One morning during his talk, all of a sudden, with a microphone in his hand he came standing right in front of me and asked furiously, "Are you free? Are you free? Tell me, tell me, are you free?" At that time I was utterly ignorant and had never experienced this way of evoking reality consciousness. So I immediately reflected and "innocently" tried to *explain* to him how free I was by *telling* him how I felt free in our community life and work. Of course, actually I was not responding to his urgent, life and death question. In everything I said I missed the heart of his challenge. Nevertheless, although it took me some time, I have come to realize how precious that encounter was that awakened my heart to the path of direct knowing.

The Move out of Eden

It is very interesting to note that for the ancient Chinese mystic, Chuang Tzu, knowledge is detrimental to human beings. He uses the words of a famous madman (mad with true wisdom) to take Confucius to task for the consciousness that classifies everything, especially as right and wrong. "Leave off, leave off this teaching men virtue! Dangerous, dangerous indeed to mark off the ground and run around (within these self created boundaries)" (*Chuang Tzu IV*). For Chuang Tzu wisdom is not found in gaining knowledge, but in returning to our primordial sense of oneness. Of course the knowledge he is referring to is reflexive, separating knowledge precisely inasmuch as it tends to block out and repress the direct, integrating

[handwritten at top: 2 think th basic Chr. experience / encounter is not intellectual, presently- / we don't come away knowing more about / something — but / rather meeting God.]

knowledge of enlightenment. So strong is he about the danger of "knowledge" that he looks at the whole process of civilization with its relationships and virtues based upon such knowledge as tantamount to the death of man's original nature. He says, "As soon as 'right' and 'wrong' made their appearance (in man's consciousness) the Way was injured. As soon as the Way was injured, love appeared (love, i.e. like and dislike, preference and rejection)" (*Chuang Tzu II*).

Does this bring to your mind the Judeo-Christian story? In it the death of man also arises out of original sin, which is described as an act of comparing and judging. Adam and Eve ate the fruit of the tree of the knowledge of good and evil! This knowing banished them from the garden where they had walked and talked with God, the boundless one. They have moved into the world of differentiating, separating knowledge. It is precisely this reflexive knowing that creates the ego. Here we can briefly note that the creation of the ego through reflective, differentiating consciousness is actually an essential step in human evolution. This is true because human perfection consists neither in the amorphic, largely undifferentiated awareness of Eden (cf. Chapter 6) nor in that blissful, limitless awareness of an ecstatic experience, but in the awareness of the boundless absolute right within the individuated perception of this tree or of this page which you are now reading. Perfect awareness is not either–or, but both–and, both relative and absolute. The ascent to the true Eden is the return to the awareness of pure being beyond all categories right within our perception of this and that and everything. As we have seen through the few examples given in the previous chapter, people can and do make this return with its accompanying feelings of limitless peace and joy.

[handwritten at bottom: nature.]

To a New Eden

question falls apart

The pattern of this ascent has been clearly presented
by Zen Buddhists for centuries. The master, Dogen, has
basically delineated the return in the famous words quoted
in Chapter 2, "To learn the path (of Buddha) is to learn the
self. To learn the self is to forget self. To forget self is to
perceive self as all things." Dogen also calls the forgetting
of self "the dropping off of mind and body" (in Japanese:
shinjin datsuraku). In this experience the ordinary awareness (mind), which is largely created by body awareness,
drops away, and "the self is perceived as all things."

From his own experience another Zen master, Wei-
hsin, presents this ascent even more clearly:

> Thirty years ago, before this aged monk (i.e. I) got
> into Zen training, I used to see a mountain as a
> mountain and a river as a river.
> Thereafter I had the chance to meet enlightened
> masters and under their guidance I could attain
> enlightenment to some extent. At this stage when
> I saw a mountain: lo! it was not a mountain.
> When I saw a river: lo! it was not a river.
> But in these days I have settled down to a position
> of final tranquillity. As I used to do in my first
> years, now I see a mountain just as a mountain,
> and a river just as a river.[1]

First there is the ordinary differentiating experience of
mountains and rivers. The suffering concomitant with this
separated state leads one to move to awareness of reality as
such without categories, i.e. no mountains or rivers. This,
too, is not a fully balanced state, so the pilgrim moves on to

the experience of all things (mountains and rivers) just as they are, within which the experience of the light of reality itself is known. The process is a dialectic in which the first two contrasting states reach synthesis and truth in the third state, the middle way.

Being Being Being!

Finally we come to the most difficult point of all when one attempts to write about enlightenment. Up to now we have gone along with the ordinary usage, "awareness of reality." But "awareness *of*" belongs only to subject-object reflexive knowledge. Enlightenment is pure awareness. It is not "of" anything. This difficult point is perhaps best elucidated by the concrete example of the inner training of Zen.

Both of us belonged to the Zen group which was started by Yasutani Roshi and then flourished under Yamada Roshi. The first practice one is usually given, in the system of training followed in this group, is counting one's breath. After some time of this the practice is changed to "*mu.*" (Mu is a negative prefix in Japanese such as un- or in- in English. But in the practice it is used as a non-meaning syllable.) This begins by concentration *on* "*mu,*" which is nothing more than an interior sound one synchronizes with each exhalation. Such concentration is difficult, because there is nothing here for the imagination or intellect to work on except this one syllable. There is nothing to be aware *of*. Gradually the inner sound "*mu*" becomes less and less some *thing* that one concentrates *on*. More and more it becomes a kind of focal point in which one's whole being is *absorbed* in each breath—*Mu! Mu! Mu!* This is what the Zen master means when he/she urges us again and again to *become one with mu.*

It is in this state that the final breakthrough occurs. Enlightenment arises. A light, as it were, turns on. This is Self-realization and every-being-realization. This is reality. Our awareness before this experience is seen to be a mistake, unreal. Self and each thing *just as it is* is seen in the light of being itself. In fact, this light is being itself. There is no distinction between light, awareness, being. There is not pure awareness *of* being but only awareness/being. Awareness *is*. Being *is*. These are not two separate categories. Awareness is being, being is awareness. That which *is* is all there is. If you want to put it in subject-verb-object form you can say there is just being being being.

Words are totally inadequate here, but we can get some help from the word so often used regarding enlightenment, i.e. realization. To realize means both to bring to concrete existence (I realize my goal) and to become aware (when I saw her face, I realized she was sick). The same word is used for existence and awareness, because ultimately these "two" are one.

Of course, what we are trying to do here is impossible, because we are using categorical words to talk about that which is beyond categories. But as long as we are doing it, we might as well go all the way and end with an outline to appease our inquiring minds. Some new elements are introduced here. Most of them will be developed in subsequent chapters. Enlightenment is:

1. direct, non-conceptual,
2. experiential, not abstract,
3. experience of the formless within forms, and of forms within the formless,
4. beyond subject-object relationship,
5. such that knower, knowing, and known are one,
6. non-comparing, non-judgmental,

7. such that all things are perceived as ultimately one and equal,

8. the self-directed flow beyond the controlling, manipulating self,

9. natural to all humans, unfolding spontaneously, not achieved by struggle and tension,

10. not exclusive, but all-inclusive, while recognizing individuals as such,

11. totally certain, without any doubt,

12. such that it flows naturally into compassion, love.

4. By What Name Shall I Call Thee?

The everlasting Logos
is born anew each day.
Where? Wherever someone
has cast his Me away.

—*Angelus Silesius*

The sixteenth century Spanish nobleman Ignatius of Loyola had been living for months in a cave near the town of Manresa in northern Spain. Doing severe penance and spending hours each day in prayer he had had an extraordinary number of visionary experiences, not only of Jesus, but also of Mary and other saints. It was Sunday morning and he was walking along the bank of the Cardoner River on his way to mass. There, by the river, gazing at the water, he had the greatest experience of his life. Years later, not long before he died, Ignatius told his biographer that he had learned more in those brief minutes than in all the other spiritual experiences and all the studies of his entire life. What, then, was this experience? What was it like? What did he see? But Ignatius could say nothing! It was not a vision. There was no voice or anything like that. All he could say was that after that he was able to "see God in all things!" Here we have it—the direct experience of God. This is true enlightenment because it is inexpressible.

Certainly St. Ignatius of Loyola here joined innumerable men and women of both east and west in the one, simple, basic reality—experience. He has no words like emptiness, *sunyata,* thusness, or tao with which to express

41

the event. He is not in a culture in which the non-conceptual is supreme, so all he can do is express nothing but its
effects in his life. He has experienced the God beyond all
categories, so now he can feel and taste this living God in
everything, in every category of being. Looking at his experience through eastern eyes we must say that Ignatius has
simply experienced being as such. He truly saw the concrete individual reality of the flowing water, and in this
seeing, the light, being itself, turned on for him. So the
experience of being as such is the experience of God. ?

In this chapter we wish to begin to look more closely at
Christian spirituality (the Christian path) under the light of
the eastern insights briefly presented in our first three
chapters. More and more we feel that through the impact
of far eastern enlightenment, Judeo-Christians can find
within their own heritage these very same insights. Often
these insights are buried beneath mountains of mental con-
ceptualization and partisan polemics. We will try to point
out the shape and make-up of these mountains, again using
contrast with the eastern path.

We are drawing especially upon Mahayana Buddhist
and classical Taoist insights. We are convinced that this
eastern influence can invigorate and be a real part of the
present day drive in the Judeo-Christian tradition to a
more mature spirituality. Our purpose is not in the least to
urge westerners to move from their path to any eastern
one. Rather, we sincerely hope that through contact with
these eastern insights many of the west will be inspired
both to rediscover the similar riches often hidden in
Judeo-Christian spirituality and to develop this path into a
better human instrument toward the fullness of life.

What Is God Like?

T: I have a very dear friend who is a true companion on the path. When she was still a little girl growing up in her native country, her mother, a Christian, began to teach her some simple prayers. She tried to teach the child to begin her prayer with the usual salutation, "O good God." But, amazingly enough, her little daughter resolutely refused to call God "good." "How can one call God good?" she insisted. How can one call God anything?

This little story brings us to the fundamental question we took up in Chapter 1: "What is God like?" As we have seen, the basic answer that the far east offers to this question is *silence*. The eastern concept of God is no concept. Only a path is presented—a path that leads to nowhere, to silence. This very silence about God teaches most powerfully that the mystery of life which the west calls "God" is truly beyond all categories—inexpressible. The path, though, is very concrete, clear and highly developed. It is a spirituality that culminates in a oneness beyond and within all relationship. At the same time it preserves existentially the individuality of everything. Recall again the basic formula in Chapter 2: "Form, this is emptiness. Emptiness, this is form." Form is the myriad of individual beings. Emptiness is inexpressible reality. They are one.

If this is actual reality, then has not this mystery been experienced and somehow expressed in the Judeo-Christian west? The answer to this question is an unequivocal yes. However, we must admit that the most prevalent Christian, western answer to "What is God like?" is actually a catechism of dogmas *about* God and a path that leads no closer than to a *relationship* with God. On the other

hand, there is ample evidence in western tradition of the
experience of God as ineffable. And this experience has
been communicated, even though there is a question
whether as of today either theology or liturgy adequately
transmits this experience.

The Inconceivable God

"I am the Lord your God; you shall not have strange
gods before me." This is the common abbreviated form of
the first commandment given to Moses on Mount Sinai
(Ex 20:1–6). The wording in scripture includes a command
not to make carved images or a likeness of anything for
worship. The Hebrews took this prohibition very seriously
and never made any image of a "god," including the Lord
their God. The second commandment is "You shall not
take the name of the Lord your God in vain." Again, the
Hebrews followed this prescription so seriously that they
resolutely refused to even utter Yahweh, the name revealed
to Moses in the desert, using instead the word *Adonai*
(Lord), or sometimes simply Heaven. Such extraordinary
reticence about the identity of God in the Hebrew tradition
is rooted in the mystical experiences of Moses and the
great prophets. These Hebrew mystics experienced to
some degree the true, living, beyond-all-categories God.
This mystical Jewish tradition continues even to this day.
In his novel *Book of Lights* Chaim Potok has a young
rabbi say:

> They say things in those books [the Kabbalah]
> that no one dares to say anywhere else. I feel com-
> fortable with those acceptable heresies. God origi-
> nally as sacred emptiness; ascents to God that are
> filled with danger. . . . [1]

These first two commandments express the non-categorical nature of divine being in very concrete ways and practices.

Of course, the Hebrew scriptures are full of anthropomorphic writings about a masculine God who gets angry, repents, rewards, and punishes, but the divine foundation of these passages is experienced as beyond all such anthropomorphisms and is simply "I AM." In Exodus 3:14 Moses' profound experience of God is expressed in this divine name. According to the text, when Moses asked to know the name, i.e. the identity, the innermost reality of God, the answer given was "I am who am." This name is a form of the verb to be or to happen. There are various translations and explanations of the phrase. According to Martin Buber the verb here has the meaning, "I will be present." W.F. Albright and other scholars take it as "I cause to be what is." But ultimately it seems that the name is intended to be cryptic and mysterious. What is clear is that God's name does not include good, powerful or any other such defining characteristics. God is simply being within and "above" all beings. This simple, mysterious meaning is further brought out in the text when Moses is told, "Say to the people of Israel, I AM has sent me to you!" The form we use nowadays, YAHWEH, is the third person form of this name, thus, HE WHO IS. Here, then we have the source of the Judeo-Christian tradition about the experience of the God who simply *is,* who transcends all adjective categories and is immanent in all that is, the one who reigns, acts in everything that happens. All the names and verbal images such as Lord, rock, fortress, etc. that the Hebrews use in referring to God are only attempts to communicate *that* which is beyond all images and whose true name is unutterable being.

Christian Witness to the Inconceivable One

Since we will take up the witness Jesus gives in this
matter in a separate chapter, we will here only indicate a
very few representative instances of this same tradition
from post-apostolic times. In the fourth century the great
mystic and theologian, Gregory of Nyssa, in spite of all
his words, makes the same now familiar call to silence
about God. "In speaking of God, when there is question
of His essence, then is the *time to keep silence*." Gregory
clearly takes the ineffability of God seriously. This is why
he says:

> . . . But in the present text I think that silence is
> mentioned first because human speech finds it
> impossible to express that reality which tran-
> scends all thought and every concept. . . .
> . . . And he who obstinately tries to express it
> in words, unconsciously offends God. For He
> Who is believed to transcend the universe must
> surely transcend speech. He who tries to circum-
> scribe the infinite in speech no longer admits that
> he is transcendent by the very fact that he equates
> God with his speech, under the impression that
> the proper description of God is only such as his
> discourse is capable of expressing. He is unaware
> that the proper notion of the supreme Being is
> preserved precisely in our belief that God tran-
> scends knowledge.[2]

Evagrius of Pontus (345–399) was one of the most
influential of all western monastic teachers. His very practical teachings on prayer are based on the inconceivability
of God.

4.   If Moses, when he attempted to draw near the burning bush, was prohibited until he should remove the shoes from his feet, how should you not free yourself of every thought that is colored by passion, seeing that you wish to see One who is beyond every thought and perception?

11.   Strive to render your mind deaf and dumb at the time of prayer and then you will be able to pray.

117.   Let me repeat this saying of mine that I once expressed on some other occasions: Happy is the spirit that attains to perfect formlessness at the time of prayer.[3]

The witness to the "unknowable" God given in the immensely influential writings of Pseudo-Dionysius, a sixth century Syrian monk, is well known and we will not quote him here. Rather, we can move on to Thomas Aquinas, the great theologian and representative of writers about God. He clearly says: "Then alone do we know God truly, when we believe that God is far beyond all that we can possibly think of God" (*Summa Contra Gentiles* I.v.). Even more illuminating is it that at the end of his life, in the midst of writing the final section of his great work, the *Summa Theologica,* he *experienced* the very incommunicability of God.

On December 6, 1273, the feast of St. Nicholas, while saying mass in the chapel of St. Nicholas, before starting his day of teaching and writing, Thomas had an experience which he never put into words. In fact, it was so ineffable that after this mass he never wrote or dictated anything. When Reginald, his close companion, realized that he had broken entirely with his routine of more than fifteen years, he asked why he had stopped writing and teaching. Thomas replied simply, "I cannot." When Reginald insisted, he finally said, "Reginald, I cannot, because all that I have written seems like straw to me." But his friend continued to question him, and at last, Thomas, after asking Reginald to reveal it to no one, said, "All that I have written seems like straw compared to what has now been revealed to me." Thus it was that this towering intellect, this immensely influential teacher and writer, was *silenced* by one brief experience of the living God.

A century later we come to one of the most powerful witnesses of the inconceivable God, the German Dominican, Meister Eckhart.

> When you come to the point when you are no longer compelled to project yourself into any image or to entertain any image in yourself, and you let go of all that is within you, then you can be transported into God's naked being.[4]

He counsels:

> One should love God mindlessly, without mind or mental activities or images or representations. Bare your soul of all mind and stay there without mind.[5]

So strong is his drive to transcend that Eckhart confesses, "I prayed to God to rid me of God."[6] He clearly teaches that God is not an *object* of our knowledge and that the experience of God is beyond relational knowing.

we are not wholly blessed, even though we are looking at divine truth; for while we are still looking at it, we are not in it. As long as one man has an object under consideration, he is not one with it. Where there is nothing but One, nothing but One is to be seen. Therefore, no man can see God except he be blind, nor know of him except through ignorance, nor understand him except through folly.[7]

A century later the experiential witness of St. Catherine of Genoa is found both clear and striking.

I see without eyes, I understand without mind, I feel without feeling, and I taste without tasting. I have no shape nor size, so that without seeing I see such divine activity and energy that, beside it, all those words like perfection, fullness and purity and that I once used now seem to me all falsehoods and fables when compared with that Truth and Directness. . . . When the creature finds himself cleansed and purified and transformed in God, then he sees what is true and clean. This sight, which is not seen, cannot be spoken or thought of.[8]

We could go on presenting testimonies to the infinity of God, but we hope that what we have given is sufficient to arouse within our readers a more urgent movement toward the actual experience of the mystery. After all, to just recall these events in the lives of our brothers and sisters east and west is not enough. It is our turn now. We hope, too, that all will be inspired to take the ineffability of God more seriously in their private prayer, in public liturgy, even, and in mindfulness within daily living. This sense of God as ineffable is the basis, the fundamental principle for a new paradigm of Christianity. God is different! God is truly infinite. This enlightenment can result in the revitalization of Christian spirituality.

A Free Spirit

One of the first effects of such an attitude toward the divine is a lightness and freedom regarding all dogma. This will mean a much more relaxed kind of spirituality. We will not be so uptight about our teachings and can travel light. Within its limits dogma can be helpful. It can give a certain guidance on the path and can inspire us to greater effort to remove the obstacles to enlightenment. Also, dogmatic formulas can furnish us words with which to attempt to express and communicate experience. After all, experience is a matter of *awareness*, and both concepts and words do arise out of awareness, even though ultimately they are inadequate regarding the divine mystery because they are intrinsically limited. The effect of words all depends on the awareness of the speaker (writer) and of the hearer (reader). If the speaker speaks from enlightened awareness, words, limited as they are, can carry unlimited meaning. If the hearer is open to this light, the result can be communication, true at-one-ment. It is for this reason that Zen treasures "communication not dependent on words," but nevertheless does use words freely and without attachment.

Concepts, images and words of themselves can help us toward the door but can never take us one step inside the temple of divine presence. The true function of the mind is to give expression to experience. The conceptualizing mind is not the locus of spiritual experience; the heart (or spirit) is. Theology is not the discipline of ultimate awareness. Faith vision (intuitive grasp of reality) is. Theology is "fides quaerens intellectum" (faith seeking understanding). The most important point here is that dogmas must be used without fear or attachment. If there is lightness and freedom of heart, then even while the mind is conceptualizing, or when the imagination is full of pictures, or the mouth and ears are engaged in words, the heart can come to know God.

Certainly it would seem that exact formulations about the nature of God, of Jesus Christ and of human nature have often been so important in church history that dogmatic orthodoxy became more important than the very experience dogma is trying to express. Even in these days the head of the Vatican's Sacred Congregation for the Doctrine of the Faith is anxious over the fact that many of the faithful have lost the old Catholic conviction that in matters of faith, "There is one truth and that this truth is definable and expressible in a precise way."[9] To this all we can do is to agree that there is only one truth, but as long as we are dealing with *mysteries of* faith we have to ask in accordance with the ancient Christian tradition whether there can ever be adequate and unchangeable definition of that which is beyond definition. In this simple book, however, we do not want to enter into any dispute about the nature of dogma. All we desire is that the ultimate inconceivability of God be truly accepted and that people be free to approach God as such.

Personal God

A: Once I went with two friends to the beautiful Monterey area of the California coast for an outing. In the afternoon we visited the old mission church of Carmel.

Before leaving we found ourselves standing in the small side chapel in front of a large, elegantly dressed statue of Mary. One friend said she wanted to pray there, so we paused for a few minutes of prayer. The two of them prayed devoutly, often looking up to the image. As usual, I simply bowed my head and entered into a state of quiet reverence and gratitude without any conscious object to whom I was grateful and reverent. After a while I looked up at the statue just as my friends did and with that my praying disappeared. Next I felt embarrassed because I was different from those around me. Reflecting on all this I realized that by natural inclination I have always been somewhat of an iconoclast. Images as images have never been a part of my life. Certain images, not necessarily always Christian, do serve the function of creating a prayerful atmosphere, but beyond that they have little effect on me.

As I look back and reflect on the various kinds of prayer forms that we have used in our religious life, it is clear that highly devotional and complicated forms, such as the rosary and stations of the cross, are simply too busy for me. On the other hand, chanting of the Latin office and mass, especially in Gregorian chant, although somewhat complicated, was food for my soul precisely because of their relative unintelligibility! Again they created an atmosphere conducive to my approach to the God beyond all concepts and images. However, there are easterners whose prayer is very devotional. I recall vividly the time a classmate in religion asked me early one afternoon to go with her. Not knowing what she wanted, I went along willingly. She led me into the chapel and asked me to kneel down with her before a statue of our Lady. I must say that that is where my willingness ended. I did kneel down, but I did not pray. Interiorly there was only a strong sense of embarrassment. It simply wasn't me!

By saying all this I do not mean that there is no devotion in my life. I do truly enter into reverent bows and gestures, into simple chanting and the lighting of incense; but strictly speaking, there is no clear object of this devotion. It is *non-relational.* In this sense it is transpersonal. As I experience it, this form of praying transforms me into an embodiment of the ineffable God. I also feel that I am very eastern.

Against this background let us take up the question of God as person. For the vast majority of Christians today, if asked what God is like, the immediate response will be to say, "He . . ." Such a response implies that God is conceived of as a person. We are very conscious that this is a delicate question, but, as we have said so often, we must take the boundlessness of God seriously. Does the inexpressibility of God extend even to "his" personhood? The answer from the east is a simple yes. "Person," too, is a category. Then, if *ultimately* we cannot classify God as a person, does that mean that "he" or "it" is impersonal? No, this too is a category.

To call God a person is clearly to put "him" into relationship. Whatever we mean by personhood, it implies an individual in relationship to other individuals. And relationship demands some kind of separation. The sense of I as person is created by the sense of you and it. Without the other we would not be aware of the self. If we had no awareness of separation from other persons and things, there would be no consciousness that this is *my* action. There would only be the sense of action pure and simple without any "my" attached to it. In the present state of the evolutionary development of our human consciousness,

mine means not yours, not its. Actually, when we call God
a person we are bringing "him" into our relational frame of
reference. Our ordinary consciousness knows only the *relative* world. The awareness of this world sees all beings as
individual, separate but inter-related. This means that we
have made the absolute (free from all limits) into limited,
relational being. Such anthropomorphization of God can
actually be a great help along the human path, but for the
moment let's insist on what the east sees as its inherent
dangers.

The fundamental danger lies in the fact that *attachment* to this human way of conceiving the divine easily
results in a wall of separation from the living God. This
separation is intrinsic to what we call a person. Thus God
as person inevitably and always remains the other. Any
spirituality that *clings* to God as a person remains para-
lyzed before an unbridgeable gap with God on the other
side. Again, such spirituality can never come to true loss of
the separate self. As long as the other remains, the self
remains. Only when the other disappears is that separation
lost. In such an attitude toward God the divine-human
union that Christians rightfully desire and claim as the goal
of life is ultimately impossible. Remember that personal
always means relational and relation always means separation. The east says that although it is a helpful approach,
personal relationship with God is not the reality we call
transpersonal oneness.

Another way of presenting this fundamental disad-
vantage of considering God as a person is found in the
experience of responsibility. When I ask myself "Who is
breathing?" or "Whose breath is this?" my intention is that
this questioning will lead me to an experience of the transpersonal self beyond all categories. However, if God is a
person truly separate from my breathing self, then how is

God involved in my breathing? If we, God and I, are two persons, then my breathing is only my action. Asking "Who is breathing?" will never take me to God. But if God is transpersonal being as such, then my personal action along with every other being is nothing but the manifestation of God. This has been the experience of all the mystics. Mechtild of Magdeburg (1210–1280) says, "The day of my spiritual awakening was the day I saw—and knew I saw—all things in God and God in all things."[10] To find God as outside all categories, even that of person, is the only way such awakening can take place. Only then is my breath truly experienced as God's breath.

Finally, there is the problem that anthropomorphizing God as a person, even as a kind of superman, actually goes against an instinctual intuition deep inside the human heart. There is a sense that somehow such a God is too small and unreal. Because of this, many reject God entirely. This rejection is a totally unnecessary tragedy. It can be very helpful to approach God as a person; however, we should always keep ourselves open for growth beyond this limit.

Radical Commonality

We have found it very helpful to express the reality of God as our radical commonality. Starting as we must with our relational world it is philosophically clear that every relationship demands two or more entities (persons or things) that are distinct but united in one common point. The fact is that all of us are constantly looking for these points of communion with other persons and even with things. When you start talking with the person next to you on the plane, one of your first questions will probably be, "Where do you live?" If, for example, the answer is "San

Jose, California," you can smile and feel a tiny sense of communion because you can say, "Oh, I used to live in San Jose, on the Alameda near Santa Clara." Your neighbor becomes more animated, and says, "Oh, I used to go bowling up there on the Alameda every Tuesday night." So as your conversation proceeds you enjoy it increasingly because you are finding more and more points that you have in common.

If you were able to enlarge these points of communion not just to huge categories like male or female, and even human being, but even beyond, you would end up at that commonality that is beyond all categories, i.e. simple being itself. All persons and things must end by saying simply, "I am." If we take delight in finding little points of agreement like living in the same town and doing similar things, imagine the joy and bliss that are possible when one existentially experiences the one commonality of all persons, things and events. This is the "I AM" Moses met. This is the God we are focusing on in this book. Radical commonality is one possible answer to the title of this chapter, "By what name shall I call thee?"

5. Traveling Light

A bag on the left,
Another on the right.
I put down all the bags,
How at ease I am.

— *The Monk Budai*

T: It was in the recreation room of the Jesuit Language School at Kamakura near Tokyo about twelve years ago. I was standing there talking with two other Jesuits when I remarked to them something like, "My loyalty to the church is no longer determined by my loyalty to canon law." When I said this, something inside me changed. I still observe canon law, but with freedom and no fear. Then, about five years after that, I remember saying to a Jesuit seminarian and to others that my loyalty to Christ no longer demanded rigid loyalty to church dogma. Again fear had dropped off and I felt free. I believe that I had put dogma in its true place. Finally, a couple of years after that, I knew in my heart and could say to one or two like-minded people that the whole approach to God as person no longer seemed right *for me*. I didn't quite know what to make of this new movement within me. Less and less was I able to truly enter into the words of the liturgy so often addressed to God as a person. I felt free, and I knew that something true was developing within my awareness, but at the same time I seemed to be moving free from the almost universal Christian position of relationship to God. It took almost three years to regain my balance, but I can now again join my heart with others at the liturgy when we pray, calling God "Father." After all, we call God absolute being, rock

57

and fortress. Even more so can we use the title Father or Mother or Lord, because these personalist images accent intelligence and love, and it is these manifestations of being that we most want to experience. Actually, just like everyone else, I, too, need personal relations in my religious search. Fortunately, to accept in all simplicity the God beyond all categories in no way takes away the reality of Jesus of Nazareth as a personal manifestation of God, and this is all I need.

I truly feel these shifts in my awareness are all of a piece with the "God is different" light that hit me there on that roof one September morning (cf. Chapter 1). I am learning to travel light. However, I sincerely believe that such liberating shifts would never have occurred had I remained all my life in the U.S. and had not experienced the influence of the far eastern awareness, especially the very awareness that Sister Agnes exemplifies in the next personal account.

A: About ten years ago, at the end of a long week of hard work during our provincial chapter meeting, we used our last ounce of energy to organize a picnic to give thanks and to celebrate the tri-annual get-together of our sisters. While we were enjoying ourselves talking, singing and laughing, I was very much taken by the harmonious spirit permeating everyone everywhere. With a deep sense of joy and contentment I quietly made a remark to the sisters sitting around me, "It is so wonderful that we work and play together in such great harmony!" A few weeks later I received a correction about the remark I had made at the picnic from a young postulant, who, it happened, was having difficulties about staying in our community. She told me quite frankly that that afternoon she was disturbed on hearing my remark. She asked my why I had not said,

"Thanks be to God for this beautiful and harmonious event." Instead, I referred directly to only what was there, what was happening right then. A few days later the postulant left the community and finally entered the Carmelite Order. When this young lady told me about her disappointment upon hearing my remark, my instinctive response was, "Oh so—I am sorry. I did not mean to disturb you." I accepted her remark and saw the validity in her trouble about my utterance. But at the same time I was fully aware that the problem fundamentally lay in my not relating to God as a person. Because of this I simply do not use God language. What drew me to Christianity and baptism was the person, Jesus, the Christ.

As I reflect on this little event, I can say that my remark at the picnic not only exposed my own ordinary awareness, but also that of an extremely large number of easterners. Prayer, for example, is not *to* God as a person but is simply a vehicle for our transpersonal religious sense. Someone once asked me what I actually mean when I pray, "Our Father in heaven . . ." I responded that I truly offer this prayer with all my heart—however, not to a person as such, but as a way to bring my state of awareness closer to the mystery of that which is, beyond all words. I would like to ask others of both east and west to reflect on what they themselves are actually saying when they pray, "Our Father . . ."

In this book we are not teaching some new doctrine foreign to the heart of traditional Christian teaching. Being totally sincere, we feel that, under the impact of eastern insights, we are only developing what is already within the teaching. The following quotation from an excellent, up-to-date presentation of Catholic theology is very revealing.

Is God "a person"? We are not asking here the question of the Trinity, whether there are three Persons in the one Godhead. We raise instead the question whether God is a separate Being among beings. Putting the question that way, the answer is "Of course not. God is not a person because God is not any one thing or being." But if the noun person is taken analogically, the answer has to be different. Does the reality we name "God" have qualities which we also attribute to persons? Yes, insofar as we understand persons as centers of intelligence, love, compassion, graciousness, fidelity and the like. What we mean by the noun God certainly must comprehend such qualities as these. In other words, it is better to attribute "personality" to God than to deny it entirely and to look upon God as some impersonal, unconscious cosmic law. And yet the attribution is always analogical; i.e., God is like a person, but God is also very much unlike a person. In the end, the revelation of God in the person of Jesus Christ must tip the balance in favor of attributing personality to God than of denying it.[1]

We were so happy when we found Father McBrien saying that God is not "a separate Being among beings," "not *a* person because God is not any one thing or being." Also, we can only agree that it would be most unfortunate "to look upon God as some impersonal, unconscious cosmic law." This, too, would be to put unqualified being into a relational classification. Finally, we recognize very well that although there are inherent difficulties in the personalist approach to God, it nonetheless has many advantages and is clearly the usual Christian approach. We fully accept it even though for ourselves we prefer the transpersonal God.

Advantages of the Personalist Approach

This approach starts from where most of us are, i.e. in a very relational state of awareness. Basically we see all persons and things in their relationship to ourselves. We see everything as pleasant or unpleasant, safe or dangerous, helpful or damaging, good or bad, etc. in regard to self and those people and things that self values. It is very natural to extend this mental attitude to God, that which we somehow experience as the very source of ourselves, our being. Devotion to God as person is a classical human path. There is a difference, however, in east and west. For the western Christian this path of devotion, often joined with the path of good works, has held almost exclusive sway, whereas in the east a third path far more direct and formless is also widely recognized and practiced.

Another point of great convenience in favor of a personalist approach is that it fulfills our need for someone to rely on. "Cast your care upon the Lord" (Ps 55:22) echoes strongly in many, many human hearts. In the midst of the unpredictable, often threatening, unmanageable circumstances of human life we can find security in the unchanging wisdom and strength of a loving God. God becomes the ideal person to whom we can give ourselves in total trust and devotion. Such a religion is easy to understand and fits a very great number of people. Actually, we ourselves feel that devotion to the personal manifestation of God in Jesus of Nazareth is fully adequate to satisfy this very human need for relationship. Ultimately, though, the per-

sonalist, devotional path itself goes beyond itself to the
light of unqualified being in which all relationships are
found to *be* in the transpersonal that which is.

What are we to say of the way Jesus calls God "Father"? The whole New Testament seems to be built around
this image of God. Certainly for the people he was teaching, Jesus had to *say* something about God. He uses the
word *Abba,* Father, to present God as the loving source of
life intimately ruling our lives. This is clearly a personal,
devotional term. As such it reflects and develops the religious sense of the Jewish people. Jesus' message was primarily given to the Jews of his time in words that fit their
mentality. To all of this the east would say that just as
"Father" is not to be taken strictly and literally, but simply
to indicate that God is like a father, so as a personalist term
it does not *define* God awareness but is a skillful means to
bring us to the risen consciousness of oneness in God.

As we mentioned in the first chapter, the ancients used
a thorn to take out a thorn. So, too, does Jesus use a thorn
of relational, categorizing consciousness to take us beyond
it to the experience of the living, infinite God. Many people today say that were Jesus still physically speaking to,
say, European or American westerners of this age, he
would substantially modify his expression. The fact is that
no matter what category we put God into, including the
category of person, we run into difficulties. For this reason
even the west has a strong apophatic (beyond speech) tradition in Christianity, in which one finally puts aside all
images of God, even verbal, in order to find the living God
in a "cloud of unknowing."

The Trinity

Within such a transpersonal experience of God what would the east say about the Christian doctrine of the Trinity, the three persons in one God? We feel that basically the east very much agrees with this Christian insight and also that again eastern intuition in this matter could help Christians to enter into the very experience that the trinitarian doctrine endeavors to express. Christianity teaches that divine life is actually a flow of life from the Father to the Son. This flow is the Spirit, so, as we humans see it, there is a Trinity. Furthermore, all life, all being, is nothing but a manifestation of this one divine life, so everything is trinitarian. This is a very dynamic expression of that which is. Precisely because it is a dynamic we feel that the east heartily agrees with such an understanding of reality. At the same time it would consider the word "persons" not as indicating three distinct and subsistent relations, but simply convenient, existential terms to express the inexpressible.

As we see it, the earliest experiential insights of Chinese philosophy are "trinitarian." These insights are beautifully transmitted in Lao Tzu's *Tao Te Ching*, which can be translated as *A Treatise on Life Power*. *Tao* is usually translated as way, but let us listen to what Lao Tzu himself says about it in his Chapter 25.

> There was a thing, a "gathering" formlessness,
> Which existed prior to heaven and earth.
> Silent! Empty!
> Existing by itself, unchanging.
> Pervading everywhere, inexhaustible,

It might be called the mother of the world.
Its name is unknown, *God or reality*
I simply call it *tao.*

Tao, then, is simply being itself, life itself, precisely as formless. It is inexpressible. "The *tao* that can be expressed is not the unchanging *tao.*" Right after making this statement in his first chapter, Lao Tzu gives two other terms to somehow present his existential insight into *tao.* These are *wu* and *yu.* When he views the ultimate, the *tao,* as inexpressible and transcendent, he uses the term *wu* (void). When it is viewed as manifested in each of the myriad of individual beings, the term used is *yu* (existent). *Wu* is formless and of infinite potential. *Yu* is *wu* concretized in an inexhaustible number of individual manifestations. The one dynamic, creative movement of *wu* manifesting as *yu,* Lao Tzu calls *te* (power).

It would be most delightful to quote more words directly from the inspired text of Lao Tzu, but we are only trying here to make the point that in this ancient eastern intuition of reality, a trinity is seen: *wu,* the unnameable origin of all; *yu,* "its" manifestation in innumerable forms; *te,* the one flow of *wu* into manifestation. These form a trinity very much like the Christian teaching. The Father is the origin, the source of all. But as Jesus says, the Father is "hidden" (Mt 6:18) and can only be seen in the Son (Jn 14:6,9). So, too, *wu* is only known in "its" manifestation *yu.* The Son is called the Word. The Father, infinite silence, speaks the Word. This speaking, this breathing of the Word is the Spirit, which, of course, means breath. Here the parallel of Spirit with *te,* the *wu*-into-*yu* movement, is obvious. Also, the Spirit is the oneness, the love of Father and Son, just as *wu* and *yu* are united in the one act, *te.* (For a further discussion of these ideas see Chapter 10.)

A similar trinity can be seen in the Buddhist teaching already quoted above: "Form is emptiness; emptiness is form." Form is the Son and emptiness is the Father. The *is* of these "two" is the one flow of life, "their" Spirit. This is where "they" are one.

What we must insist on here is that just as any trinitarian expressions found in the east are rooted in the dynamic life experience of the ancient mystics, so the Christian teaching should be considered as a flowering of the actual experience of the early Christians under the impact of the life and presence of Jesus of Nazareth. Also, we are very conscious that the theological doctrine of the Trinity is far more complicated than the little we have presented here. All that we intend is to indicate how eastern intuitions can give fresh impact and reality to an often obtrusively presented trinitarian expression of the mystery of life.

Traveling Light

T: I remember the time I went for a walk and a talk with Lorca in the hills of Kamakura, Japan. She was a young American of Catholic heritage searching in the Zen halls of Japan for truth and inner freedom. As we talked she insisted that she did not want to be tied down to any fixed teachings or set system of training. She was very sincere in this. It was not an unwillingness to make sacrifices and embrace real discipline. Rather there was something deep inside her telling her that truth is beyond all boundaries and that freedom is only in unfettered infinity. Basically I agreed with her and told her so. At the same time I pointed out that it is helpful to talk about the boundless with, albeit, limited words and that any discipline is followed only so that we can go beyond discipline.

As to dogmas and discipline, then, let us travel light, happily using our intellectual and ascetical heritage without fear, inhibition or attachment. Let our attention be not on intellectual explanations, but on mindfulness of the existential experience of flowing water, living trees, struggling humans and all the forms of that which is. Let us return to the silent contemplation of our daily life events. We cannot but agree with the common insight that all true philosophy and theology must end in silence, the fruitful silence of life experience. Again we quote *Tao Te Ching,* "Returning to the root comes to be silence: this is the restoration of life" (Chapter 16). We can conclude with the famous poem of the Chinese poet, Tao Chien (373–427).

> To live in the midst of people
> And not to hear the noise
>   of cars and horses,
>
> How could this be possible? . . .
> A detached mind creates a quiet place.
>
> Gathering chrysanthemums
>   under the eastern hedgegrow,
> Silently gazing
>   at the southern mountains,
>
> Beautiful mountain air,
>   setting sun,
> Birds flocking, returning home . . .
>
> There is something in all these events.
> Yet,
> When I try to express it,
> I become lost in no words.

                          (authors' translation)

6. Mist-aches

Our mist-aches come from a deluded heart
Misted by the fear-fettering lie
   that God is apart from us.

Hazed by the guilt-giving illusion
   that Eden has never been supplanted *[handwritten: good.]*
      by Easter.

Yes, our mist-aches come because we mis-take
the dream for the reality,
   the illusion for the fact,
Eden for Easter, the Lie for the Light.

   —*Joan Metzner, MM*[1]

From all that you have read in this book, you may
have already realized that what we are actually doing is to
gradually lay the groundwork for a new paradigm of the
Christian philosophy of life. We sincerely feel that in the
evolutionary thrust of human consciousness there is a new
frame of reference emerging, within which quite a number
of Christians will be able to more appropriately see and
understand our world. *[handwritten: Tho I think they may be surrendering certain basic truths of Xianity a Sib relign—that]*
We conceive of this new paradigm as an essential part
of the advance and evolutionary revitalization of Christian
spirituality. Also, we are convinced that influence from
eastern spiritual paths must play an important role in this
development. On the other hand, we see this new conceptual framework as a growth of seeds and plants already
rooted from the very beginning in western Judeo-Christian
traditions. We would also stress that we truly do not offer

this new paradigm as an entirely new replacement for the traditional one. In the great sweep of the Christian path we would propose it as more fitting to some people than to others. We affirm a plurality of Christian spiritual paths and hope that we can all walk together in our various ways within the great way, Jesus, the Christ.

So far we have presented this emerging paradigm as one that takes the infinity of God seriously. In fact, the entire framework is built on the existential and radical limitlessness of the divine. This paradigm fully accepts the psychological approach to God as person, but on the other hand does not see God as a separate reality "out there." Rather, it sees God as the absolute commonality found in all relationships, person to person, person to thing, thing to thing.

We can now turn to some of the implications of this approach to God and to our human development. We will continue to follow the middle path of giving full reality to "both" the absolute and the relative, the one and many, with no separation between "them." We are writing this book as Christians and, as such, Jesus of Nazareth is the focal point of our consideration. His very name Jesus (Jehoshua) means "Yahweh saves." Jesus is primarily our savior. What does this mean? How are we saved by him and from what? In other words, we need to honestly understand our human condition, and what there is in it from which we need to be delivered. We can begin this further elaboration, the groundwork, of the new paradigm, then, with a discussion of the problem of our human situation as presented in the second and third chapters of Genesis. What is the real meaning of the Judeo-Christian myth of original sin?

When "I" Was Frightened

A: Ever since I became a Christian the myth of original sin has intrigued and puzzled me. Why does God forbid the first parents to have the knowledge of good and evil? What is so wrong with this knowledge that God does not want humans to experience it? The popular Christian interpretation of the Bible story somehow seemed rather superficial to me. Light was thrown on the subject by a frightening experience I had during the year when a sister and I were renting a house in Berkeley while attending classes at the Graduate Theological Union.

One afternoon we were working in the yard. At the end of our work, while I was heading to the back yard to put away the tools we used, out of nowhere a big tall man appeared in front of me. I was so utterly scared that I simply stood face to face before him and could neither talk nor move. He must have noticed my helplessness, for immediately he said, "I am looking for a black cat. Did you see a black cat?" I don't remember how and what I responded to his question. But this incident so shocked me that I was frightened for many days. I started to ask myself why I was so scared and by whom I was really frightened. Then I realized it all came from my differentiated, separated and judgmental consciousness. At the moment of my meeting with the unexpected visitor, I habitually, instinctively, judged him as bad and threatening. It was "I," my own separated self, that had frightened me. I am sure that if I had operated with enlightened consciousness, I would have been able to handle the unexpected situation with serenity and even friendliness. But I failed to do so because I was still living in and operating out of an "original sin" consciousness.

Human Predicament: Christian Understanding

Utilizing the creation account given in Genesis 2–3, the traditional Christian analysis of our human predicament is that, in the beginning, human beings were created in a state of beautiful purity and happiness. They lived in a garden of Eden (i.e. of delight). They walked and talked with a personal God. This God commanded them not to eat of the tree of the knowledge of good and evil. Into this paradise entered the clever serpent who is the tempting villain and is later cursed by God. Eve followed the serpent's suggestion and then led Adam into eating the forbidden fruit. The result of this disobedience was that the two were expelled from Eden. This is called the fall from the original state of innocence and from right relations with God. All suffering and even death are seen to be the result of this fall. In fact, all our present problems are ultimately considered to be a just punishment for this primal disobedience. Despite the many questions and obvious problems inherent in this analysis (i.e. Why should we suffer now for their sin?), this basic explanation of our human situation has generally held sway to this present day.

Just as the problem is rooted in the disobedience of the one man, Adam, so the solution is found in the obedience of the one "Son of Man," Jesus of Nazareth. We are saved by his obedience even to death on the cross. By this sacrificial death God is appeased and humankind is restored to God's good grace—in fact, to an even higher level of sanctifying grace than before the fall. "O felix culpa—O happy fault, O necessary sin of Adam, which gained for us so great a Redeemer!" (Easter Vigil liturgy).

Far Eastern Understanding

The far eastern (especially Mahayana Buddhist and Taoist) analysis of our historical and present human situation contrasts quite sharply with the Christian viewpoint. Very little, if anything, is said of an original state of innocent happiness. Also, we must say that the sense of a personal God is nothing like the way it is in the west. Nor is there any real sense of disobedience to the command of this God. Suffering is held to arise from ignorance and "salvation" is basically a process of awakening to what is real. The teaching of enlightened masters, especially that of Buddha himself, points out and draws humans to this awakening in which the fundamental goodness and potential of human nature is realized.

An Evolutionary Understanding

One of the most serious challenges to the traditional Christian paradigm of the human situation has been the scientific evidence for evolution. On the other hand, the evolutionary analysis of human history fits quite well with the far eastern consciousness. Actually, as we see it, evolution sheds immense light on the Genesis creation myth. So much is this so that we will join the evolutionary view together with insights from the east to develop for Christians a new understanding of the human predicament. As we proceed we will follow in general the saga of human evolution as outlined in the brilliant works of Ken Wilber, especially the superb synthesis of many disciplines he presents in *Up From Eden*.[2] For the actual proof of the brief outline we present, we can only refer to Wilber and to the sources he synthesizes. Wilber presents three large divisions of human development: 1. sub-conscious, pre-personal; 2. self-conscious, personal; 3. super-conscious, trans-personal. He breaks the three down into eight major divisions. The hierarchical structure of these eight, rising from the ground unconscious up to the absolute consciousness, he calls the Great Chain of Being. For our purposes in this chapter, we will mainly use the triple division, which we would also like to indicate by the terms: 1. uniformity; 2. individuation; 3. unity. These stages can be found within the evolution of human society in general and in the life movement of each individual human.

To begin with, then, human evolution is actually a process of growth in consciousness. Evolutionary physical changes are clearly oriented toward higher and higher levels of awareness. It is within the context of levels of awareness that the paradise of Genesis is to be situated. Wilber argues convincingly that this paradise was not that of fully realized human beings, but rather a very primitive, infant-like state of awareness which knew nothing of the complexity and fears of modern consciousness. As human beings arose into the lower stage of the Great Chain of Being, perhaps as early as five million years ago, they had a consciousness far different from that we "enjoy" today. It was a pre-personal state in which they had no separate egos, but lived with little if any separation from the great flow of nature. Man was undifferentiated from, embedded in, fused with, in a sense, confused with the material world. This is stage one, the stage of uniformity.

It is exactly this awareness that the psychologists of infancy say is the consciousness of a newborn baby. Piaget says that, in an infant, the world and the self are one. For the first four to six months there is no awareness of individuation. This is a non-relational state of perception. But as an infant bites its thumb it feels the thumb in its mouth

and some pain in the thumb. However, when it bites a
blanket, it has feeling in its mouth but not in the blanket. It
has a different experience. Just as an infant grows in a
sense of its body as individuated from all other bodies and
things, so the "dawn human" gradually developed an
awareness of its own body as distinct from others.

The next step toward individuation is on the emotional level. Take, for example, an infant who is crying and
sees that its mother is smiling or laughing. In this situation,
the infant develops a sense of "my" emotion as distinct
from the emotion of others. This same process continues
on into the mental realm of ideas and values. The child and
then the teenager moves step by step away from its parents
until it is able to stand apart and distinct as an individuated person. Again, all the anthropological and cultural
evidence confirms that this has actually been the evolutionary development of humans out from a clearly pre-
personal state of awareness right up to the highly individuated, independent person of the modern world. This we
call stage two, that of individuation.

The development of the human ego is by no means the
full realization of the potential that is inherent in the
human species. It is only a major step on the way to the
third stage, that of union. As we moderns are painfully
aware, along with the process of individuation and the
growth of self-identification there also arises simultaneously a natural longing for that union which will over-
come the sense of separation and isolation concomitant to
individuation. Again it is to be noted that there can be no
union unless there is self-identification. The state of union
is not a return to the uniformity stage in which all are
numerically one, but a state in which a plurality of true
individuals is united in a shared commonality. This commonality is not found in the sharing of a numerical, but of

a non-categorical one. As is obvious, it is this non-categorical absolute, unqualified one that Buddhists refer to as the
"void" and Christians call "God."

Today the average human consciousness is by no
means in the state of union, but is still struggling and suffering in the second stage. However, there must have
always been individuals who are at the advance edge of the
evolutionary thrust. These "saints" show us clearly the
various levels within the unitive stage toward which we are
all oriented.

Eden Revisited

In this paradigm of human development we do recognize that there was a kind of Eden state that lasted for an
immense length of time. There is a certain bliss in the
consciousness based in the numerical oneness of stage one.
However, for centuries the Christian interpretation has to
some degree confused this pre-personal security and bliss
with that trans-personal union which human nature is oriented toward. The fall from Eden is not really a fall but a
rising to a higher level of individuated consciousness.
Using the very passage we traditionally consider as an account of a fall and a regression, let us examine more carefully this critical stage in human evolution, because this
truly is where most of us are.

To begin with, the cunning serpent of Genesis is not
really the villain, but the hero of the event. The serpent is
the ancient symbol for the consciousness thrust of the
human life force. The dawn human was *immersed* in the
subconscious realms of mineral, vegetable and animal life.
In this state there was only the very slow emergence of
mental reflection, verbal representation, and conscious relationships. With so little separation, there was no anxiety,

[handwritten margin note at top: 2 their their own "real" own". Even as an evolving "ape-man" — not the fall creating]

no shame, no real comprehension or fear of death. It truly was a kind of garden of Eden (delight). The symbol for this early hominid awareness is the ancient mythic serpent eating its own tail. The serpent (consciousness) is moving around at the ground level without raising its head to see. In those days, there was what we can call *human* consciousness, but it is dominated by the subconscious world of mineral, plant and animal. Matter is conscious but only of itself. Yet this very material being has the potential to rise stage by stage up the awareness ladder from material awareness to image to mental to soul to spirit, until there is spirit aware of spirit in all the operations of the lower areas of the great hierarchical Chain of Being. This rising consciousness power is called the serpent power. Of all the powers in the human animal the consciousness drive is the most "spiritual." "Now the serpent was the most cunning of all the animals" (NAB Gen 3:1; RSV: "most subtle"). It took many millennia after the evolution of the first hominids, but the serpent did gradually *raise its head,* as its very nature demands. Consciousness began to rise beyond its domination by matter. It advanced through the highest pre-personal subconscious stage up to the early mind, verbal, personal stage, then on to the advanced stage with its self-reflexive, relational ego consciousness. In other words, humankind was moved by the serpent power to leave the pre-personal garden of Eden as a necessary step up the evolutionary ladder. It was not a fall, but a rising. Not an exile, but a step toward home.

[handwritten margin notes: Serpent is the ground mental consciousness of man. 76 devil be comes god. ?]

Naked and Ashamed

In this new state of awareness our ancestors discovered the separation of the many. They are no longer aware only of a vague oneness, but have come to experience their individual separation. This would seem to be the meaning of Adam and Eve finding that they are naked. In their consciousness they are no longer clothed with the whole material world but are separated from it. This causes shame because they now are instinctively conscious that they are not where they should be. They are no longer clothed with uniformity and are not yet in the conscious state of unity.

Another level of interpretation might be that there is shame because humans with their new elevation of consciousness now realize how much they are still dominated by matter and physical instincts. Feeling the pull to rise to the freedom of spirit consciousness, we are ashamed to still be so limited by matter consciousness. In their shame Adam and Eve try to cover themselves with fig leaves. Since this embarrassment is because of the power of matter over us, and since the materializing power is ultimately located in the first, the genital energy center (*chakra*), it is natural that these parts must be covered over. Again recall how an infant has no such embarrassment. The shame only arises fully as a human person grows to individuation and ego development.

But clothes are not our only cover-up. In a sense, anything that we use to hide and alleviate our naked and embarrassing separation is to be placed under the fig leaves symbolism. Perennial examples of these fig leaves, of our attempts to relieve this isolation, are the possession of property and things, control of people and events, even all levels of human relationship. However, none of these substitutes will save us (make us *whole*) unless within them we awaken to our existential oneness in the absolute (God, void).

Fear and Death

With the raising of the serpent power Adam and Eve are conscious and reflexive enough to stand back from the flow of life and judge things and events as good or evil. Before this, humans are simply aware of the constantly changing flow of life, of which they are a part. Now through consciousness they establish an "I" that is outside, but in relation to everything else. It is this "I" that judges all as good or evil in reference to itself or something it values. Humans have truly become "like gods," because their emerging mental powers have actually created and now rule a world of their own with the ego as the center. The inevitable clash of individual egos (ideas, wills, values, desires) breaks the pre-personal uniformity and lays us open to anxiety, fear, envy, and struggle, even violence, against one another (Cain against Abel). The greatest fear that arises is that of death. Standing more and more alone and still building its individuation largely on body separation, the ego's greatest felt danger is the loss of the self through bodily death. ". . . for in the day that you eat of it you shall die" (Gen 2:17). This can hardly mean that before the rise from matter dominated awareness humans did not die. Rather, physical death was simply a part of the one great changing process called nature, with which they identified *themselves*. However, after their consciousness rose, the transformation called death was looked on as *the* threat to their individual ego world. Before, death was just a part of the flow of the one life; now it is feared as the very termination of the ego that has been so laboriously arrived at. Clearly, today, the greater the ego, the more intense is the avoidance, rejection and fear of death. On the other hand, for the person whose ego attachment has been reduced through the discipline of meditation and of life itself, physical life and death are seen as one continuous process of development.

The better way to see death

Punishments

As humans advanced into the self-conscious, personal stage, they became far more judgmental and began to realize the predicament they were in. We have already seen that the Genesis myth judges this advance of awareness as an expulsion from a garden of delight. This expulsion is done by the Lord God and is presented as a punishment. In this new judgmental awareness women come to look upon the labor and dangers of childbirth as another of the punishments. "To the woman he (God) said, 'I will greatly multiply your pain in childbearing; in pain you shall bring forth children . . .'" (Gen 3:16). Probably we can say that the very anxiety brought on by advanced consciousness also causes the birth process to become more tense and difficult. In Adam's case he becomes critically aware of the unpredictability of nature and of his own need to toil to control nature's growth process. These difficulties, too, are judged to be divine punishment. "And to Adam he said, 'Because you have listened to the voice of your wife and have eaten of the tree of which I commanded you, "You shall not eat of it," cursed is the ground because of you. In toil you shall eat of it all the days of your life. . . . In the sweat of your face you shall eat bread till you return to the ground, for out of it you were taken; you are dust and to dust you shall return'" (Gen 3:17,19). So death itself is the last and greatest of the punishments.

Finally there is the overpowering symbol of the cherubim and the flaming sword. "He (God) drove out the man;

and at the east of the garden of Eden he placed the cherubim and a flaming sword which turned every way, to guard the way to the tree of life" (3:24), ". . . lest he (man) put forth his hand and take also the tree of life, and eat, and live forever" (3:22). In our interpretation, this tree of life at the center of the garden can only mean the very spirit itself which gives life to all beings. It refers to the infinite force immanent in the whole evolutionary movement of this world. When spirit is aware of spirit within our awareness of all creatures, we discover (enter) eternal life. But this final stage, the stage of unity, is blocked by cherubim, who guard sacred places and access to divinity itself, and by a flaming sword. This is the flame of purification and the sword which cuts away the exclusive, small ego; for without this purification there can be no realization of self and all beings as God in manifestation. And the cherubim will not allow humans dominated by categorical consciousness to approach the true God, who is beyond all categories.

A Christian Insight

Before concluding this chapter it must be noted that the validity of our position regarding the human predicament does not depend upon the somewhat detailed interpretation of the Genesis text which we have just made. The details of the exposition are certainly open to discussion. For example, our interpretation of the symbolism of the fig leaves and the flaming sword is only presented as consistent and most plausible. We sincerely hold, however, that the basic thesis of humankind's gradual advance in consciousness through the three general stages is firmly based upon the scientific data of physical, emotional, mental and spiritual evolution. For an excellent discussion of all this data we again refer you to Wilber's books.

We can also note here that even within the traditional Christian interpretation of Genesis, the "fall" into differentiating good and evil consciousness is regarded as a great boon to humanity. The final result is seen to be that we have been lifted to a much higher level of grace. It can well be argued that ultimately this higher level is not too different from the rising of humanity which is presented in our paradigm.

We conclude with some words of the great Russian Christian mystic, Nicolas Berdyaev. Writing of Eden he states, "Paradise is the unconscious (state) of nature, the realm of instinct. There is in it no division between subject and object, no reflection, no painful conflict or consciousness with the unconscious."[3] As to the "fall" he continues:

> Man rejected the bliss . . . of Eden and chose the pain and tragedy of cosmic life in order to explore his destiny to its inmost depths. This was the birth of consciousness with its painful dividedness. In falling away from the harmony of paradise . . . man began to make distinctions and valuations, tasted the fruit of the tree of knowledge and found himself on this side of good and evil. The prohibition was a warning that the fruits of the tree of knowledge were bitter and deadly. Knowledge was born out of freedom, out of the dark recesses of the irrational. Man preferred death and the bitterness of discrimination to the blissful and innocent life of ignorance.[4]

Berdyaev clearly recognizes that the "fall" is not a fall when he says: "The myth of the Fall does not humiliate man, but extols him to wonderful heights. . . . The myth of the Fall is a myth of man's greatness."[5] Finally, he is very clear about the three states of preconscious, conscious and superconscious.

> After the Fall ... consciousness was needed to
> safeguard man from the yawning abyss below. But
> consciousness also shuts off from the supercon-
> scious, divine reality and prevents intuitive con-
> templation of God. And in seeking to break
> through to superconsciousness, to the abyss
> above, man often falls into the subconscious—the
> abyss below. In our sinful world consciousness
> means, dividedness, pain and suffering. ... Un-
> happy consciousness can only be overcome
> through superconsciousness.[6]

How then are we humans to move from this difficult stage up to the superconsciousness of the longed for unity? This we take up in the next and ensuing chapters.

7. True Emptiness—
Wondrous Being

> Christ was born a man for me,
> For me He died—
> Unless I become God through Him,
> His birth is mocked, His death denied.

> —*Angelus Silesius*

A: Many times I have been asked to tell my story of becoming a Christian and ending up as a Catholic nun. Some people ask directly, "How did you become a Christian?" or "Why did you become a nun?" Others address the same question in more complicated ways, such as "What does it mean to you that Jesus is your savior?" or "What does salvation mean to you?" Every time I have to answer these questions of ultimate personal concern I always go back to a movie I saw in my early teens. It was a Japanese film, "The Bells of Nagasaki." After the terrible bombing of the city there were many orphans facing the unbearable sorrow of separation from their dead parents. I cried bitterly throughout the whole show. I simply couldn't bear the sight of children without their parents. After this a secret desire was born in my heart, "When I grow up, if I have the money, I want to build an orphanage." This innocent ambition stayed and grew within me as the years went on. Then I heard the story of Jesus of Nazareth from my Christian friends. That he died as a criminal, although totally innocent, intrigued me. Who is he? What does his life and death mean? One simple truth about Jesus Christ was clear to me at that time—that Jesus was a selfless

83

person who lived his whole life for others. His death, too, was for others.

Here my desire to live for others born of "The Bells of Nagasaki" was reenkindled and strengthened. I felt that the melody of Jesus' life was just what was the deepest part of myself. His life and death at-one-ment were so powerful and magnetic that I could not help feeling attunement with him and I ended up a Catholic and a nun. I didn't reason it all out, but I knew instinctively that his selfless way of living and dying was the path to heal all wounds of separation in the world, especially that of children from their parents.

This personal account brings us directly to the next major part of this book. We have considered God as infinite. We have examined self, the loss of self and enlightenment. Finally, having investigated our present difficult stage of evolutionary development, we must now meet Jesus, the Christ. As humans we must answer his question, "Who do you say that I am?" (Mt 16:15). What is his place in the saga of the realization of our human potential?

Jesus, the Christ: Light of Life

In general, we can say that the east, both Christian and non-Christian, sees Jesus of Nazareth as a truly enlightened person. To put it in the words of our new paradigm, he is felt to be at the advance edge of the evolutionary thrust. He is a human hero who has gone ahead of us and one who can lead us to our true fulfillment. In fact, his first disciples experienced and described him as having entered into the perfection of the third and final stage, that of unity. Jesus says of himself, "I am the light of the world; the one who follows me will not walk in darkness, but will have the light of life" (Jn 8:12). This "light of life" brings to

mind "the tree of life." Both phrases refer to the same
reality, to the one awareness/being that gives existence and
life to our whole cosmos of beings. Jesus can say "I am the
light of the world" because he has endured the total purification of the flaming sword guarding the tree of life. His
ego has been so purified of mis-take and illusion that he has
eaten of the tree of life, has entered eternal life and is now
the "light of life." His very self-identification, which is
"both" individuated and all-inclusive, is the light that can
bring us to experience the whole world as it is, as many *and*
one. He joyfully proclaims that if we follow him, i.e. put on
his self-identification, we will be enlightened: ". . . you will
know the truth and the truth will set you free" (Jn 8:32). It
is because he is the embodiment of light that he is to be
seen as our savior.

To Be Saved?

Life can be described as existence in unity. Before
examining *how* Jesus of Nazareth shows us the way to
unity, to life, we must clarify some general ideas about
salvation. Recall the traditional paradigm of a personal
God offended by the disobedience of humanity both in the
"original sin" and in all personal sin since then. Humans
are seen to be out of God's good grace and therefore must
do something to atone for this break and thus restore good
relations with God, even to a higher level of sanctifying
grace than before. This theory of salvation reached a kind
of clarifying climax in the teaching of St. Anselm of Can-
terbury (d. 1109). He argues that since God is infinite in
dignity, disobedience to God is an infinite offense and
demands infinite reparation. However, humans are finite
and can never perform an act of infinite dignity. So God in
his unlimited mercy and love sent his own Son to become

human. As God made flesh he offered a sacrificial act fitting to the divine dignity. In this act we are all saved. Jesus has taken all the punishment due to us and redeemed us (bought us back) by his blood.

This salvation theory is still very common in the Christian consciousness. We find expressions of it all throughout our present liturgy. Sunday morning TV and radio broadcasts proclaim it incessantly. It rests on many biblical expressions, on a certain kind of consciousness that can be found in many, if not all, cultures and on sharp scholastic reasoning. Certainly this theory of salvation has helped millions over the centuries and will continue to do so. However, we would like to point out a different one, not to cancel out the traditional, but to stand beside it as another option for serious Christians. As always, this option arises from an eastern viewpoint. Simply put, we would like to say that salvation is not so much a matter of redemption, as en*light*enment. This theory, too, is rooted in scripture (as has been briefly indicated earlier in this chapter). Also, it is clearly found in Christian tradition. (One example that comes to mind is that one ancient name for baptism is illumination delivering us from the powers of darkness.) Finally, it is in accord with the theory of consciousness evolution which we have been following and with eastern consciousness in general.

Although the word salvation is not so acceptable to some moderns, basically it is an excellent word. Its Latin root is *salvus* (safe), which is related to the simpler form *salus* (health), which in turn is related to the Greek *holos* (whole, holy). So to be saved is to be safe, which is found in health, which is basically wholeness or holiness. To be whole is to be saved. Or as some people would say, when we get it all together, we are truly healthy and happy. Salvation, then, has to do with entering into wholeness, into unity. The unity at the end of evolution is different from the uniformity at the beginning in that the individual consciously remains. Our present, common state of awareness is not an illusion except in that it is sadly and fearfully incomplete. We make a mis-take about things. We are already in unity. We don't have to become whole; we already are. It is our over-individuated consciousness that deceives us into our fearful feeling of isolation. All that is needed in order to enter unity and be saved is to discover that all our realities are from the beginning one in the radical commonality we call God. This ultimate *metanoia* (change of awareness) is salvation.

The east prefers to use the word liberation. This is not just liberation from delusion and all the grasping attachment and suffering born of delusion. It also means freedom in the sense of unlimited and unrestricted. In the state of true freedom a person experiences all things, and especially self, as the unlimited one, God, *in manifestation.* Christian tradition calls us humans the glory of God. Salvation is to discover that this our life *is* eternal life.

Jesus, the Christ, as Savior

Each one of us, as an individual manifestation of unrestricted being, must open his/her eye of awareness to experience reality. No other individual can do this for us. How, then, can anyone be a savior for others? Specifically, how is Jesus, the Christ, actually our savior?

Imagine a large wall filled with a great number of clocks. They are all pendulum clocks and are all made to beat to a certain rhythm. But as you look at the clocks you can see that they are off-beat. Each one is doing its own

thing and not one of them is completely in tune with its
own being. Therefore, each one is out of tune with all the
rest. Everything is disharmony and cacophony. Now, suppose that you take another clock of the same kind as the
others, but one that is running strongly just as it is made to
run. You put it in the middle of the wall. The wall itself is a
connection and at first the off-beat clocks try to draw the
new clock into their various rhythms, even though it is the
nature of these clocks to beat together. But The Clock resists all such temptations. Gradually, the clocks nearest
The Clock are drawn to entrust themselves to its True
Rhythm, because, actually it is their own natural rhythm.
This entrustment leads to attunement, and attunement to
the experience of at-one-ment, which is salvation. The delusion of separate existence and its false advantages is
gone. All clocks are free to be themselves because of the
influence of The Clock which is true to its self.

This is the process which Jesus of Nazareth refers to
when he says, "When I am lifted up (on the cross and then
in resurrection), I will draw all to myself" (Jn 12:32). The
title that Jesus consistently gives to himself is "Son of
Man." Although this does seem to refer to the Son of Man
figure in the prophecy of Daniel, nevertheless in both Old
and New Testaments we feel that this title presents Jesus as
the very embodiment of the true human being. He is
"everyman." When any human being fully opens the self
out to Jesus, the truth of that person's being is actualized.
This entrustment of self to the enlightened one, Jesus, is
what we call faith. In Christianity the actual entrustment of
faith is based upon the memory of Jesus' life, death and
resurrection. Above all, it is in his suffering, death and
resurrection that Jesus draws us to the full realization of
our inborn potential, to salvation.

This book, tho strange to western Xcain, may actually provide a way, however, for Easterners to cross th bridge over to Xcainity.

Jesus' Death to Self

The cross is the central point and culmination of the
life of Jesus. It is not just its termination, but the event to
which everything is directed. In Luke's gospel we see that
the adult Jesus makes only one journey to Jerusalem and
this for the purpose of suffering, dying and rising. "As the
time drew near for him to be taken up to heaven, he resolutely took the road for Jerusalem" (Lk 9:51). Jesus is fully
aware that a fearful event of self-emptying is ahead. He
says, "I have a baptism to receive; how distressed I am
until it is over" (Lk 12:50). This baptism is his suffering
and death. Until he goes through this self-emptying he is
constrained by the conditions of the empirical world and
categorical self.

Our ordinary human ego is constituted by and perceived in relationships. In the relative order, I am I due to
relationship to the other. This other is experienced both
horizontally and vertically. Our horizontal relationships
are all those we have with human beings and everything
else around us. Our metaphorical relationship with God
can be said to be vertical. This relational way of considering God and self is not strictly correct, but we will use it for
the sake of an easy to follow presentation. His suffering
and death is the process by which Jesus emptied himself of
all relationships, both the existential horizontal and psychological vertical, and thus died to self.

Here, we must again note the connection there is between our self-identification and our body consciousness.
So closely is our ordinary human selfhood connected to
body awareness that in English we constantly use the word
body to indicate the self (somebody, nobody, she is a kind
body). Thus we can say that the destruction of the body

constitutes a large part of self-emptying. The scourging of Jesus, the beating, the loss of blood, the carrying of the cross and the crucifixion itself all amount to the destruction of Jesus' body. They are also his way of dying to self. The actual event of the suffering and death is not just an interior experience but a full embodiment in space and time of Jesus' journey into emptiness. In it he experienced and manifested the process of his categorical disidentification, his loss of the relative self.

Horizontal Kenosis

The actual process of Jesus' loss of his self-creating human relationships began with Judas' betrayal. Jesus was betrayed by one of his chosen friends. Then he was denied by the chief disciple, Peter, and finally *all* deserted him. "Then all the disciples left him and ran away" (Mk 14:50). (John did return at the end but we will give our interpretation of this below.) In this desertion Jesus experienced and manifested the loss of his self-identification in the category of master and teacher.

After the betrayal, Jesus was officially tried by the representatives of the Jewish people and expelled to die *outside the sacred city.* By this rejection he was stripped of his identification as Jew and messiah. However, the actual sentence and execution was done by the Romans, who effectively represented the whole world (cf. Lk 2:1, where the Roman census is described as a census of the whole world). This complicated event of total rejection meant that Jesus could no longer find himself as a member of his nation, race, religious tradition or even of this whole world. It was his "hour to go from this world" (Jn 13:1).

Nor could he find himself to be part of the most fundamental human relationship—family. When Jesus says,

"Woman, here is your son," he is not just telling Mary to look to John for home and support, but at the level to which his consciousness has reached, he is saying to her, "*I am outside the category of 'your* son.' " He is manifesting the detachment process that carries him to a self-awareness beyond even this most intimate relationship of son to mother. To John he says, "This is your mother"—"she is not my mother because I am beyond such categories now."

Finally, at this deeper level, we can interpret the stripping of his garments as an expression of the shedding not only of material possessions and the self-identification that is often found in them, but even of all the horizontal relationships which constitute human selfhood. We feel that this is the way we must read even such traditional statements as Walter Kasper's,

> . . . for the New Testament Jesus' death is not just the doing of the Jews and Romans, but the saving act of God and Jesus' voluntary *self* sacrifice.[1] (emphasis added)

Vertical Kenosis

Jesus' uprooting went further and deeper than the horizontal dimensions. Both Matthew and Mark give as the only words of Jesus on the cross the mysterious cry, "My God, my God, why have you abandoned me?" Scripture scholars say that by quoting the first words of Psalm 22, Jesus is claiming the fulfillment of this psalm in himself. Other scholars and mystics, while not denying this interpretation, go deeper and hear them as a cry of profound emptying. We would agree, and take them as Jesus' experience of the ultimate *kenosis*. Here he is undergoing the final loss of that categorical self which is found in its metaphorical relationship to God as person. God is no longer *The Other,* but simply the infinite, and Jesus is infinitely open. It is this openness to the infinite that he expresses in his words, "I thirst" (Jn 19:28). It is his arrival at the threshold of the complete and perfect transpersonal break-through that he attests to in his final words, "It is accomplished" (Jn 29:30). This total kenosis is well expressed in the words of the modern theologian, John Cobb:

> To be empty is to lack any boundaries, any determining content of one's own, any filter through which the world is experienced. To be empty is to be perfectly open to what is there, whatever that may be.[2]

The great Flemish mystic, Ruysbroeck, when speaking of "the God-seeing man," says, "His spirit is undifferentiated and without distinction, and therefore it feels nothing but unity."[3]

"I solemnly assure you, unless the grain of wheat falls to the earth and dies, it remains just a grain of wheat. But if it dies, it produces much fruit" (Jn 12:24). So, at last, as both the horizontal and the vertical arms of the cross vanish into that central point of no dimensions, Jesus bursts forth into the fullness of life—the resurrection.

Resurrection

Now using all our insights so far as a background, let us look closely at the data about the experience of the risen Christ as given in the New Testament. In the gospels especially we find that just as Jesus used bodily death to show his total emptying of self, so he used his bodily resurrection to proclaim his entry into the fullness of self-realization.

Here it can be objected that the gospels give us only a brief and even confusing account of the resurrection. But modern scriptural scholarship has vigorously pointed out that the gospels are first and foremost the expression of the experience of early Christians. The evangelists use the historical events of Christ's life to present the first Christians' faith experience of the risen, living Jesus. Most scripture authorities say of all the gospels that the intention of the authors was to produce a document not of history but of divine experience. These documents are filled with the light of the resurrection. Throughout, it is primarily the risen Jesus who is portrayed.

This presentation of the resurrection of Jesus is even more clear in Paul and the other New Testament letters. Here it is not the historical events of Jesus' life, but the daily life of Christians that is used to present the new life in God, the risen state.

"He Is Risen"—Life

As the title of this chapter we chose the Zen saying "True emptiness is Wondrous Being." We have briefly discussed Jesus Christ's entry into true emptiness beyond all categories. Now we must take up the mysterious state of being he is in in the eternal now. Of course the first thing to say is that *he is alive*. Resurrection means return to life. This is certainly that fullness of life he himself speaks of: "I came that they might have life and have it to the full" (NAB Jn 10:10). This life is the spirit life that vivifies the whole world. Countless sages and enlightened ones down through the evolutionary ages have in varying degrees experienced this life force. Our description of the actual life of Jesus right now must perforce remain quite speculative, but we can gain some idea of it from the experiences of these great spiritual giants of our race. For example, take the Chinese mystic–philosopher, Chuang Tzu. His writings (especially the first seven chapters) are an astonishing testimony towering above all those we know of in the ages around him except for those of his fellow Taoist, Lao Tzu. So far is he in advance that it seems that very few could really follow him and no lasting spiritual path built on his enlightenment remains. (Taoists might object to this statement. The history is very uncertain.)

In chapter six, Chuang Tzu speaks of the truly enlightened person as one who "plays (or wanders) in the one breath of heaven and earth." Breath here (in Chinese—*chi;* in Japanese—*ki*) is the life-giving force, the spirit, that gives being to every person, thing, event in the whole universe. Its manifestations are the categorical myriads, but "it" is beyond categories. The life of a person who perfectly experiences this total void/total being is carried along by the power and purpose of this force, so that he/she is playing. There is only effortless effort, just power, wisdom and love manifesting itself. In this playing life there is no fear, anxiety, effort, real suffering or real death. There is only the fullness of Life, ever ancient, ever new.

Through his existential experience of suffering and physical "death," Jesus went beyond all categories. He, in effect, said I am not this, I am not that, until the only experience left was that of only I AM, pure being. The "I" of the unqualified "I AM" is transpersonal. It expresses non-categorical life beyond and within all space and time. It is eternal life. Jesus experiences that ultimately there is no death, that life is simply "changed, not ended" (Preface, Funeral Liturgy), that everything is only eternal life in temporal manifestation.

By entering into awareness of this life force a person discovers his/her identity with it. In other words, it is through awareness that we enter eternal life. Christ Jesus teaches this ultimate "beyond death" reality to his disciples by emptying the tomb of his physical remains and freely manifesting to them in bodily form. In the "one breath of heaven and earth" there is unlimited power. Jesus can now freely materialize himself at any time, any place that he wishes.

"We Have Seen the Lord"—Power

Having said that Jesus is in the fullness of life, we have actually said everything about his present state. However, another fundamental description of the early Christians' faith experience is "We have seen the Lord." (The word *Kyrios* [Lord] and its Semitic equivalents, *mar* and *adon,* indicate legitimate domination and power and originally meant "Master," or, more strongly, "Sovereign.") As this title tells us the early disciples experienced Jesus as a being of total power and dominion. When Paul met Jesus on the way to Damascus he was knocked to the ground and blinded by the immense energy of the being encountered. Again, when Jesus poured out his Spirit upon the disciples at Pentecost they were filled with the divine energy and strength that carried them to the ends of the earth. Finally, we see this power and dominion of Jesus clearly connected with self-emptying in the ancient hymn of the letter to the Philippians, "He emptied himself. . . . Therefore God has highly exalted him . . . and every tongue should confess that Jesus Christ is the Lord" (Phil 2:5–11).

A very important law operates in the process of self-emptying or the process of disidentification. Philosopher Ken Wilber states this law succinctly: "By *differentiating* the self from an object, the self *transcends* that object and thus can *operate* upon it."[4] For example, if I identify myself with my emotions, I am my emotions and as my emotions change I am under their control. But if I realize that I am not my emotions, that I *have* emotions, then the liberated *I* can take responsibility for them and control them. I am *lord over* them. If this process of realizing that I am not this or that extends to every category of being, then I have and control every*thing*. I am lord of creation. This is the self Jesus expresses in Matthew 28:18, "All authority in heaven and on earth has been given to me," and this is the Jesus that faith experiences.

God, I AM, is quite literally the power being manifested in all phenomena. This power is of infinite potential. Jesus is now the perfect manifestation of I AM. That is why Thomas, when he saw and truly experienced the presence of Jesus in the upper room one week after Easter Sunday, cried out, "My Lord and my God." The I of pure I AM is clearly the Lord of all.

"Abide in My Love"

These words testify to the experience that the disciples had of Jesus' abiding presence with them, which, of course, is a presence of love. That the risen state is a state of pure love is our next point in this exploration. All love is relational. In every relation there are two entities, e.g. two persons. These two (or more) are related in something common to them both. When this commonality is discovered, the two experience love. Again, let us return to the "I AM" consciousness. It is this pure, non-categorical being that is common to everything. When this is discovered, one enters into love of all beings and this love is unconditional and unchanging, because the relationship is founded on being itself. Love is based upon the reality that there is only one flow of energy enlivening us all. In his resurrection

Jesus discovered with full enlightenment the commonality of his *being with* all creatures. "I *am with* you always." This existential being-with is mutual abiding. Jesus invites all to this love, saying, "Abide in my love."

"Incredulous for Sheer Joy"

In the account Luke gives of the appearance of Jesus to his apostles on Easter Sunday night, the disciples are described as "incredulous for sheer joy." The connection between joy and love is, of course, very obvious. Joy is the certain sign of true love. In fact, we can say that peace arises with the experience of order, happiness accompanies harmony, while joy comes with the experience of love. Recall the example of Hakuin mentioned in Chapter 3. Upon hearing the bell, his inner eye was opened, and he shouted out with immense joy. Of course, Hakuin knew that he was he and the bell was the bell over there, but in that very sense perception, he knew the commonality to both himself and the bell. He knew pure, infinite, common being, and this experience of communion (love) brought wondrous joy.

This is the joy that Jesus now knows in its perfection and shares with those who entrust themselves to attunement with him. He has promised to share his love and "the joy no one can take from you." This joy is always with us, because it is in every perception of reality that an enlightened heart can make.

Pioneer and Perfecter

We conclude by considering a little more deeply the great *pascha* (passage) that Jesus, the Christ has made. As always, our primary concern is what has happened to his awareness, because it is by awareness that one enters into life. Using the Bible as our source we can say that the Hebrew consciousness before the advent of the Christ rarely, if ever, went above the highest levels of the self-conscious, personal stage. This is not to say, however, that it is not advanced for its period. When Moses descended from Sinai, he brought to the people a personal God, Yahweh. Old Testament mysticism is that of communion with this God. Daily religion is in terms of a covenant between two parties. There is still subject-object dualism and always at least a subtle distinction between creature and creator.

Jesus, too, maintains this worshiping awareness when he teaches his disciples to pray, "Our Father in heaven." But in the end Jesus himself moves beyond all subject-object dualism. Both his soul and the personal God are dissolved in the void he entered through his radical self-disidentification, his *kenosis*. No longer does he simply worship and commune *with* the Father. Now he says "I and the Father are *one*" (Jn 17:22). The light (consciousness) he has entered is transpersonal, the full experience of infinity. To use Paul's words from the second letter to the Corinthians, "Now the Lord is the Spirit" (3:17). This is the divine spirit that moved over the indeterminate waters of Genesis 1 and is working and producing the great evolutionary development from the beginning. The "I" of Jesus is now all-inclusive. He says over the whole universe, "This is my body!" Paul experienced union with this Jesus and can therefore cry out, ". . . it is no longer I (the exclusive self) who live, but Christ who lives in me" (Gal 2:20).

However, as we see it, although the "I" of Jesus is no longer exclusive and isolating, but inclusive of the whole cosmos, it still remains individuated, because ultimately there is no opposition between spirit and matter. To put it in other words, forms are the formless and the formless is forms. As an individuated human being, God in manifestation, the Nazarene is still Jesus; as Christ, the anointed, he is infinite spirit. To use the ancient formula, Son of Man, Son of God.

In Hebrews 12:2, Paul tells us to persevere in the race, "looking to Jesus the pioneer and perfecter of our faith." Truly he is our pioneer who has gone ahead to the never ending completion of evolutionary development. As Christians we are to entrust ourselves (faith) to his ever present influence and he will bring this faith to perfection. "I will come again and will take you to *myself,* that where *I* am you may be also" (Jn 14:3; italics added). The actual experience of some of those who have entrusted themselves to him bear powerful testimony to the truth of his promises. We present them just as they are quoted in Wilber.

"My being is God, not by simple participation, but by a true transformation of my Being. My *me* is God."

—*St. Catherine of Genoa*

"See! I am God; See! I am in all things; See! I can do all things!"

—*Dame Julian of Norwich*

And best of all:

"The ground of God and the Ground of the soul are one and the same."

—*Meister Eckhart*[5]

Hopefully, the brief overview given in this chapter of the journey of our hero, Jesus of Nazareth, has already brought up again the next obvious question, "How are we

Idet 2

to actually follow Christ?" Each one of us is rightfully concerned about our own journey and how best to join Christ
within "the reign of God." Our succeeding chapters, then,
will all deal with our following of Christ. As always, the
presentation is from the perspective of eastern paradigms.

8. *At the Foot of the Mountain*

The divided, ascending
Paths at the foot of the mountain
Do differ, but
We all <u>see the very sa</u>me
<u>Moon at the summit.</u>

        (Authors' translation)

        ∽

Wakenoboru
Fumoto no michi wa
Kotonaredo,
Onaji takane no
Tsuki wo miru kana.

      —Nitobe Inazo

    This poem of the great Japanese Christian Nitobe
Inazo brings to mind a trip we made to Mount Hiei just
north of Kyoto. In 1987 both of us were privileged to attend a stimulating conference sponsored by the World
Council of Churches on "Spirituality in Interfaith Dialogue." It was a memorable event played out in the Kyoto
hills amid autumn colors mixed with even a morning
snowfall. One afternoon we were all driven up to visit the
great complex of temples and spiritual practice halls of
Enryakuji, the headquarters of Ten Dai Buddhism in
Japan since its foundation in 788 A.D. The Most Venera-
ble Yamada Etai, the abbot of over ninety years of age,
welcomed us with a beautiful, open-hearted talk. Even
more than by our visits to some of the temples, it was

101

through a video presentation that we were given a detailed
view of the various spiritual practices carried on there even
today. The striking thing about the discipline at Mount
Hiei is its variety. Some monks are doing zazen, others
chanting mantra, others doing prostrations, a few circum-
ambulating the whole mountain in prayer (about twenty-
five miles) morning after morning for a total of one thousand days.

The severity and strictness in all this is truly inspiring,
but it is the variety that is of greatest interest to us here. In
fact, Mount Hiei is called the *bozan* (mother mountain)
because so many branches of Japanese Buddhism have
been born from there. Saints such as Honen and Shinran
(Pure Land), Eisai and Dogen (Zen), Nichiren, Ippen and
founders of other Buddhist sects in Japan spent their early
days in practice at Enryakuji. In fact, the walls of the first
temple we visited were filled with many large portraits
commemorating each of these former practitioners at this
great temple. Each one came to focus mainly on one practice and upon this built his branch. The various disciplines
are joined with differing emphases in doctrine, but they all
live and work together harmoniously on Mount Hiei, hopefully creating the founder Saicho's desire of "people who
illuminate their surroundings."

Just as it is of the greatest importance to accept a
plurality of viewpoints and spiritual teachings about God
and our human situation, so must we admit a diversity of
spiritual paths built around a variety of spiritual practices.
The paths at the bottom of the mountain of God truly do
differ. To demand uniformity bespeaks a consciousness
that is still too close to the first stage of evolution. Or, at
best, it indicates a highly developed and narrow ego which
demands conformity to itself. We must let people grow
from where they are, using disciplines that are helpful to

them. By the same token, it is essential that we know where
we are individually, adopt practices helpful to ourselves
and not waste time flitting from one practice to another
after hearing how successful some were for other persons.
However, it must be admitted that we are all complex and
changeable. A devotional person sometimes tires of images
and words. A Zen type soul can also sing a song such as
"Sometimes I Feel Like a Motherless Child." Our individual practices can vary.

It is very enlightening that the New Testament gives
relatively little about actual spiritual practices. It is wholly
centered on Jesus of Nazareth, the events of his life and the
self-identity from which he acted. Very little is said about
practical paths to sharing in this consciousness. In effect,
this leaves the Christian path open to embrace the whole
gamut of skillful means which humans have devised for the
actualization of the divine potential within.

What Do You Seek?

When discussing the fundamentals of how to actually
follow Christ, the question of intention naturally arises.
This is the start and foundation of everything in the matter
of the spiritual path, because without an intention that
fully grips us we will never persevere. And speaking even
more fundamentally, our intention determines the focus of
our attention and what we are attentive to decides what is
actualized. That which we really want happens. As the
Christ says from his own experience: "Ask, and it *will be*
given to you; seek, and you *will find;* knock, and it *will be*
opened to you" (Mt 7:7; our italics). So fundamental is all
this that the first words Jesus speaks in the gospel of John
have to do with intention: "What do you seek?" (1:38).

The scene is the River Jordan. John the Baptizer sees

Jesus walking by and says to two of his own disciples, "Behold the Lamb of God." They follow after Jesus. Then "Jesus turned and saw them following and said to them, 'What do you seek?' " If they are to truly follow him, this is the first and essential question.

T: When speaking of the matter of intention I always recall my *shoken* (formal seeing) with our Zen master, Yamada Koun Roshi. I had been in Japan for fifteen and a half years before I got up enough courage and consciousness to make the walk down the hill from our language school in Kamakura to the poor old temple, Jomyoji. It was here that one of the Zen groups founded by Yasutani Hakuun Roshi was having its semi-monthly meetings. After attending the six introductory talks by Miyazaki Sensei and having given evidence of my sincerity about zazen, I was allowed to have the formal meeting with Yamada Roshi that would make me his disciple in all things concerning Zen practice. This meeting was called *shoken*. During it there was only one thing asked and discussed— my intention.

Today, as always, people enter the Christian church for various reasons. Many are baptized as infants. When these grow up the question of intention is of paramount importance. Many "born" Catholics, for example, in childhood and early teens, go to mass and practice their religion largely because of their superego, the "I must" I that comes from the commands of parents and teachers. When they grow up and move away from parental dependence, they can easily give up the early practices, because the power of the superego is so reduced. Various motives can arise in this situation. Some continue to practice because they like the social gathering that a parish affords. Others are held in place because fear of punishment and the force of the superego are still powerful. Others find an outlet for their organizational or money-making abilities in various church activities. For quite a number, Christianity with its devotion to the Father, to Jesus Christ, and to the saints is a source of real strength and consolation. The security of a strong moral and doctrinal teaching motivates some to maintain membership.

All of these and other intentions (or a mixture of them) that bring people to the Christian path are good and by no means necessarily egocentric. However, the Christ himself rarely speaks of such motives. He even seems sad that people only come to him for healing and spectacular cures (cf. Mt 12:38; Jn 4:48). What he holds out to us as that which should move us to follow him is the truth that frees, the food and water that give life, identification with the reign of God, the fullness of life. In a word, he wants us to seek *metanoia* (a change of consciousness and energy flow).

Let us return again to that meeting with the first two disciples. "Jesus said to them, 'What do you seek?' and they said to him, 'Rabbi (which means Teacher), where are you staying?' " On the surface this can be taken as a request to know the tent, cave or house in which Jesus is physically staying. But the gospel of John, above all, deals with symbols and archetypes. In fact, this very section is at the beginning of what today is called the book of *signs* (1:19–12:50). The whole gospel is named the "spiritual" gospel because from first to last it uses concrete events to lead us to the realization of the life force, the spirit. "Where are you staying?" then refers to Jesus' state of consciousness. As John presents these two disciples (and probably he was one of them), they have felt something in Jesus and are interested in sharing in the enlightenment of this attractive Galilean. This line of interpretation is strengthened by the formulation of Jesus' answer, "Come and *see*!" "Share in

my awareness, in my experience of reality," is what he is
saying. Jesus invites them to the truth, to life. "They came
and saw where he was staying; and they stayed with him
that day." They visited him physically, but more impor-
tantly they experienced where he was interiorly, and to
some degree shared in his light.

John then adds, "It was about the tenth hour." We can
interpret this to mean that John mentions the hour because
ten is the number of fulfillment, fullness and perfection.
Ten indicates what they found in Jesus. This point is con-
firmed by the next verses. One of the two, Andrew, "found
his brother Simon and said to him, 'We have found the
Messiah.' " The messiah is the one anointed by the Spirit,
the fully alive one. Surely this must have been a powerful,
life-giving experience for the first two disciples. They went
"and *saw.*"

From this very first encounter, this *shoken* in John's
gospel, we can see that what Christ Jesus invites us to have
as our intention in following him and as the motivation for
our whole lives is enlightenment. "Come," he says, "and
see." However, in a very real sense, if we do follow him and
grow in enlightenment, we finally end up having *no* intention. We will find ourselves with no purpose in life! On the
other hand, our lives will move even more rapidly to fulfillment. This paradox needs some attempt at explanation.
This we will try to give in Chapter 10. It will revolve
around following nature, so the quotation below from a
modern Japanese Zen master can serve as a preview of that
chapter. At the same time, since it is written for those who
are starting out on the spiritual path, it will conclude this
section of our first discussion here at the foot of the mountain. (*Unsui* means literally "cloud-water" and is a term for
a Zen trainee.)

Moving Cloud, Flowing Water

A cloud moves and water flows in selfless
    openness.
This is the heart of the *Unsui.*
Moving and flowing without any goal,
    they arrive precisely where they are
    made to arrive.
If clumsily they go against the wind and flow,
    at once the selfless openness vanishes.
To quietly entrust one's ears and eyes
    to the moving clouds and flow of water,
To learn selfless openness,
This is the salvation of modern humans.

—*Tachibana Koshu Roshi*
(Authors' translation)

Three Classical Paths

Although all spiritual paths share the same general
goal (embodiment of spirit consciousness) and means (detachment, especially from self-centeredness), the actual
concrete means and sub-goals can vary greatly. In fact, they
ultimately become very personal. As the poem beginning
this chapter says, the paths at the foot of the mountain are
all divided and different, because people are different. In
the midst of the bewildering variety of spiritual disciplines
and practices available to people today, it is essential that
each person have an existential sense of one's basic orien-
tation(s). To flit around to this workshop and that trying
out a potpourri of self-development techniques and spiritual arts is ultimately counter-productive. To make progress we must stay within the parameters of our own path.

A Taste of Water

There are many paradigms of analysis that can assist us to determine our own characteristic orientation(s). We will present here a short summary of the ancient and well-known triple division that is derived mainly from the Hindu classic, the *Bhagavad Gita.* To be sure, these three paths are expressed in western spiritual writings, but it is in the east in general and in the *Gita* in particular that they are most clearly delineated. Although we all have some of each type of energy flow, nevertheless most people are able to recognize themselves as mainly of either the *bhakti,* the *karma* or the *jyana* path. The following is a very cursory outline of each path considered under seven categories.

Before reading this section:

If you would like some help in discovering the basic orientation(s) of your own particular path, a questionnaire is given in Appendix A. If you wish to do the questionnaire, it would be best to do it before reading the section below. This will ensure a certain spontaneity and lack of prejudice. Some help towards the interpretation of the questionnaire is found in Appendix B.

A. BHAKTI—THE PATH OF DEVOTION. "I want to love."

The Lord Krishna says, "Whatever you do, or eat, or give, or offer in adoration, let it be an offering to me; and whatever you suffer, suffer it for me" (*Gita* 9:27).

1. *Main Intention:* To lose oneself in and to become one with one's object of devotion.
2. *Focal Point of Attention:* The Lord, Lady, Beloved, Master, etc.
3. *Entrustment to (Faith in):* The Lord, Master, etc. More precisely, to the spirit within the object of one's devotion.

4. *Human Powers Especially Used:* Emotions, memory, imagination. The heart energy center (chakra). However, all one's powers are engaged.

5. *Prayer Style:* Devotional. Use of memory and imagination. Repetition of the names of the Lord. Chanting. Hymns of praise and entrustment. Every practice from the use of many words, images and concepts to simply "looking at Him (Her) looking at me."

6. *Other Spiritual Practices:* Doing one's work "for Him/Her." Reading the words and life of the Lord. Liturgical gathering in the Lord's name.

7. *Dangers:* Never going beyond the relational. Relativizing the absolute. Using the other (the Lord, etc.) for personal desires, ego security, ego aggrandizement. Looking on other paths as insensitive, as not "religious" enough, and not really accepting them. Narrow attachment to various devotional practices.

B. KARMA—THE PATH OF ACTION. "I want to act, to do."

"The world is in the bonds of action, unless the action is consecration. Let thy actions then be pure, free from the bonds of desire" (*Gita* 3:9).

1. *Main Intention:* To lose oneself in *true* action.

2. *Focal Point of Attention:* This act, this work.

3. *Entrustment to:* This action; to the spirit manifesting in this work.

4. *Human Powers Especially Used:* Physical activity, practical intellect. The base, gut, and solar plexus energy centers.

5. *Prayer Style:* The various eastern "ways" such as the way of tea, calligraphy, *aikido, judo, karate.* Copying the scriptures. *Tai chi.* Pilgrimages. At the highest level: the prayer of simple doing, "My work is prayer."

6. *Other Spiritual Practices:* Acting without any desire for reward. Forgetting oneself in one's work. Any occupation or profession (teaching, nursing, shopkeeping, cabbage growing; even soldiering is mentioned in the *Gita*).

7. *Dangers:* Distracted, unfocused, shallow action. Attachment to one's work and its reward. Using work and other people for self-aggrandizement. Disregard for the absolute (for spirit). Absolutizing activity. Looking on other paths as impractical, even useless (e.g. no value to contemplative communities).

C. JYANA—THE PATH OF KNOWLEDGE. "I want to see, to know."

"When one sees Eternity in things that pass away and Infinity in finite things, then one has pure knowledge" (*Gita* 18:20).

1. *Main Intention:* To lose oneself in spirit knowledge. (Knowledge here means intuitive knowledge. Spirit knowledge sees God in all and all in God.)

2. *Focal Point of Attention:* The formless in forms, especially in self. "Emptiness, this is form. Form, this is emptiness" (*Heart Sutra*).

3. *Entrustment to:* The spirit manifesting in every form, in one's self.

4. *Human Powers Especially Used:* The mind, especially the intuitive mind. Bodily posture. Breathing. The brow (third eye) energy center.

5. *Prayer Style:* Silent sitting (zazen, dhyana). Walking meditation. Exhaustive questioning, especially "Who/What am I?" Attention without an object.

6. *Other Practices:* Mindfulness in everything. Simplification in everything. Exhaustive study of texts and spiritual teachings (using the intellect to go beyond the intellect).

7. *Dangers:* Considering the whole relative world as pure illusion. To disregard the relative. Lack of healthy concern for and contact with the relative world. Attachment to study and/or solitude. Pride in one's experience and looking on other paths as low-level awareness. Getting lost in conceptual activity.

9. On the Way Up

> Let us run with perseverance
> the race that is set before us.
>
> —*Hebrews 12:1*

T: It was during one of the darkest, most difficult periods of my life that somehow it worked out that I attended an intensive meditation retreat high in the mountains of Colorado. The retreat had brought up all the confusion I was then feeling about my life as a religious priest and as a Catholic. This darkness had been going on for many months. At the same time, it was a period of intermittent light and insights. One of these had to do with the self-emptying of Jesus Christ. (It is part of the basis for Chapter 7.) I had been expressing this series of insights by the phrase: Jesus has no name. This means that, although he is validly named Jesus, a Hebrew from Nazareth, at the same time he is the infinite, albeit the infinite in manifestation.

There were only two of us sleeping in a large camp dormitory that night. I lay there for hours tossing and turning amid a confusion of thoughts about myself and my life. As the inner discomfort increased in the darkness, I suddenly sat up in bed and looked out a window at the end of the building. There, framed by the window, was a stark, whitish cross standing out from the blackness behind. At that moment I realized that I, too, have no name! I, too, am the infinite, indescribable. Again, it was not at all a powerful burst of enlightening energy. Just a quiet insight that brought calm to my confusion and some degree of peace. It was a tiny breakthrough that expanded my self-awareness.

113

It also empowered me enough that shortly after I was able to go in all humility to a person much younger than myself and receive help that did bring new self-identification and reintegration.

The next morning I discovered that the cross that had taught me my no name reality was nothing but a weather-beaten board nailed to the thin trunk of a dead tree. The outside lighting caught it just right as one looked through the dormitory window.

This tiny event is related as an example of what happens to all of us at times, especially when we are in darkness and stress. We actually do break through to the advance edge of our consciousness development. Such experiences may not bring full integration, and we may very well slip back into narrow, confining consciousness patterns. However, they do give us some inkling of where our evolutionary drive is drawing us./In this chapter we will present a summary picture of the various stages of our human path "up from Eden," with special attention to what lies ahead as we evolve toward spirit consciousness.

Two Figures

One of the most common images of human life is that of a journey up a mountain. John of the Cross entitles his spiritual classic: *The Ascent of Mount Carmel.* In the poem quoted at the beginning of the previous chapter, the paths are placed at the foot of the mountain. They are described not only as divided but also as ascending to convergence at the summit. Having briefly discussed the divisions in the previous chapter, we will now take up their ascent, or, more precisely, the stages of ascent. Here again we will base our discussion on the works of Ken Wilber. Figures 1 and 2

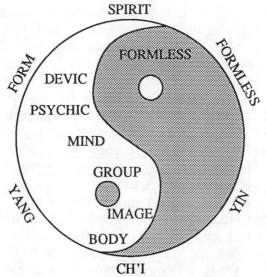

Figure 1: **CONSCIOUSNESS LEVELS**

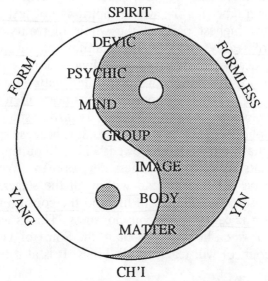

Figure 2: **ONTOLOGICAL LEVELS**

are our modified and simply amplified version of the stages of consciousness development that Wilber gives under the title, "The Great Chain of Being" (*Up From Eden*, p. 8). These figures deserve close attention because this chapter will simply be an exposition of the ideas crystallized in them, especially in Figure 1.

We can first note the points the two figures have in common. The circle as such represents all reality as we know it. This circle is labeled spirit in English and *ch'i* in Chinese. The first and most basic characteristic of reality is that it is dynamic. Both spirit and *ch'i* are names for an energy that is in constant movement. In the west it was Heraclitus (sixth century B.C.) who first discovered and recorded that reality is basically movement. He states this insight very simply, *"Panta rei"* (Greek for "All things are flowing"). Traditionally, this movement is called spirit (wind, breath). Since this describes the whole of reality in any and all forms, we have placed this term outside the circle as a label for the whole. Spirit is not just one part, albeit the highest part, of the whole of reality. It is the whole of reality and is being manifest all throughout in varying degrees of density and individuation.

It is for this reason that spirit and matter are not to be thought of as actually opposed, as has been often taught in the west. Matter is simply a dense, *relatively* static concentration of life energy, of spirit. Also, it is because spirit is all reality that we have not followed Wilber in putting spirit as an eighth stage of consciousness development. We feel that it must be put outside and within all the stages. For the same reason, the fullness of life and the consummation of evolution is called spirit consciousness. This is what Jesus speaks of when he promises that "the Spirit of Truth" (i.e. of experience) will teach us all things. It is also the reason why "all power in heaven and earth" is given to the fully enlightened. In the state of spirit consciousness we realize the one force being manifest in everything. We find ourselves as individuated everything. We are spirit aware of spirit. This is bliss.

At about the same time as Heraclitus and even before him, the great Taoist philosophers in China were also reflecting on their experience of life. They, too, discovered and recorded the basic dynamism of reality. The Chinese word for spirit is *ch'i,* which we have placed at the bottom of the circle. It was these superb Taoist philosophers of life who saw this one energy flow as composed of two ultimate principles, *yin* and *yang.* The most general terms in English for these two principles are formless and form. In actuality the spirit, which is the ultimate movement of the elemental life force, is the movement from formless to form to formless to form to . . .

Since *yin* or formlessness has absolutely no distinguishing features, we have followed tradition and have represented it as pure black darkness. *Yang,* or form, is, of course, white, representing all colors and all forms. The movement of one to the other is represented by the curving line, and since each principle is intrinsically oriented toward the other, each side of the figure contains a small circle of the other. So far, the two figures are identical and teach us the same picture of reality.

Figure 2 gives a sevenfold division of existent beings. This is our rather primitive attempt to indicate the whole gamut of differentiated (form) beings from the most elemental material manifestations up to the highest and most universal, archetypical (devic) levels. Again note that each one of these levels is nothing but the spirit movement of formless to form to formless to . . . To express this the

seven levels are placed within both the *yin* and *yang* principles. In its actual reality, an existent being is always form-
formless. We are using the term existent in its root Latin
meaning of standing (*sistere*) out (*ex*). An existent is the
formless standing out in a form. Without further explanation we will move back to Figure 1, which is our primary
concern here.

Figure 1 has to do with the evolutionary development
of *human consciousness.* The first thing you might notice
about this figure is that all the levels of consciousness except formless are placed on the form side. A further difference is found in that the "matter" level is dropped and the
level of formless consciousness is added at the top. These
changes are made precisely because this figure has to do
not with reality as it actually exists, but with what we are
aware of about reality. The first six levels are placed in the
form or categorical side because at these stages there is
usually little awareness of the formless/*yin* principle as
such. This is especially true of the lower levels. For example, when we are conscious of our bodies (level one), there
is usually only the vaguest, if any, experience of the infinite, formless/*yin* principle that is manifesting in this
body–form. At the same time, it would seem that the possi-
bility and availability of the awareness of the indescribable
infinite increases as one goes up the ladder of levels. However, it is only when we have passed through death to all
categories and forms into objectless, formless consciousness that we are able to enter into the completion of the
evolutionary journey called spirit consciousness. It is then
that we experience the formless in all levels of form and all
forms in the infinite potential of formlessness. All things
are *ch'i,* and *ch'i* is nothing but the dynamic movement of
yin to *yang* to *yin* to *yang* to . . .

Evolutionary Stages

Before taking up the various stages of consciousness development, there are two general points that must be made. First, since the origin, driving force and ultimate goal of the evolution of human consciousness is spirit, this evolution itself is the spiritual path. For this reason we find all the various advancing stages of consciousness best exemplified in the great spiritual masters of our race. Second, the various stages are established by that which dominates consciousness as a human person processes his/her life experiences. This dominating awareness has changed over the centuries of human development. Also, it changes during the course of our individual lives and even our days. As an example of the last case, say that you are immensely thirsty. Confronted with a tall glass of cool beer, you will see it simply as something to drink and assuage your thirst. Here body consciousness dominates all others. Another time, when you are not thirsty at all, you might see the glass of beer as something so clear and beautiful, as something to enjoy by contemplating it. This is mental awareness at work. Finally, if you are in a strong psychic state, you will see the beer as something to be avoided, because it would interfere with your dominant psychic awareness.

First Four Stages

The development of human consciousness begins at the body level. Although all matter is somehow conscious, specifically human awareness began with human body consciousness. This beginning is dated roughly at five million years B.C. Of course, it is a very vague, hardly differentiated consciousness. Like that of a human baby from birth up to four or six months, awareness at this *first stage* is still dominated by matter and the external senses. Self is only vaguely distinguished from the flow of matter energy. This is the age of the gatherers, who just go with the cycles of nature with almost no tools to assist them. They are fed as infants, as it were, from the breast of mother earth.

By roughly 200,000 B.C. the human brain had evolved enough for humans to rise from a life totally immersed in the senses to that in which imagination plays a major part. This is the *second stage*. Interiorly, when humans create images, they launch out into a whole new world in which they have more creativity and control. Exteriorly, the male human turns into a hunter who develops spears, knives and such tools and aggressively expands his food source. Mankind is established a bit more outside total dependence upon the cycles of nature. At the same time, mind is still dominated by matter, now not just through external senses, but also by material images in the imagination. There is an expansion of consciousness from just the material world to that of fantasy. Also, as the image world becomes stronger, it in turn dominates to some degree the material. That is why this is called the stage of magic. Finally, the earth becomes personified to some degree as the Great Mother.

This level of consciousness is like that of a human baby from roughly six months up to one and a half or two years. It is still largely a pre-personal stage. However, even from this level some shamans moved far ahead of the general mass of humanity up through mind/group and mind/ego awareness all the way to the highly expanded psychic consciousness of the fifth stage. At this second level such shamans were the advanced edge of the human evolutionary drive. Wilber points out that advance consciousness is rare and that it never seems to evolve more than three levels above the general run of human awareness.

The *third stage* began about the year 12,000 B.C.
There is clearly a growing mental activity here. It corre-
sponds roughly to a child's development from about one
and a half to three and a half or four. This is the time of
language development. With language people are able to
communicate more. They enter into the social oneness of
groups and clans. As discriminating mental activity increases, personal identity clearly arises, but this emerging
self-consciousness is dominated by the group. Social activity increases and city states are formed. Consciousness is
expanded into the much broader world of ideas and mental
categories. A real sense of time emerges. The wandering
hunter settles down to farming, a way of life that represents
even greater control of nature for the group's own purpose.
Finally, group gods appear and the Great Mother becomes
the Great Goddess.

The magical control of life through the images of stage
two is heightened to the image/mental control through
myths. For this reason this stage is called the mythic–
membership period. Note, too, that through myths humanity is given a poetic interpretation of life and a growing
sense of the mysterious formless principle underlying all
phenomena. Finally, the priests and saints of this age advance up to the highest personal level, to the archetypical
level. This represents the highest degree of form consciousness.

The *fourth stage* is that of the individuated, self-conscious ego. It is obviously a personal stage. Human consciousness has so evolved that it can now constitute an
individual subject, an ego, who is unique and separate
from everyone and everything else. Mental activity has
become very self reflective. It is also able to use not just
images but also general concepts and principles to attain an
ever increasing degree of control (for better or worse) over

our natural environment. Since this is our present stage and a period with increasingly well-documented history, Wilber breaks it down into three periods: Low Mental/ Egoic stage from 2500 or 2000 B.C. to 500 B.C.; Middle stage from 500 B.C. to 1500 A.D.; High period from 1500 A.D. to the present. Again, these stages are roughly equivalent to a child's years from four to seven, seven to twelve, and twelve to whenever (if ever) the person truly begins to move out of ego-centered awareness toward transpersonal realization. With the development of the personal ego we find increasing devotion to a personal God and the struggle against a personal Satan. Also, as the mind gains greater control over human lives and gives more freedom from the cycles of mother nature, the father form rises to ascendency over the mother (e.g. patriarchy and the Father God) and solar time begins to replace lunar. Finally, mental abstractions and generalization make possible the trading, money and banking society we are so familiar with.

It is interesting to note that it is precisely around the year 500 B.C. that great mystics arose in human history to advance awareness beyond the relative to clear experience of the absolute within the relative. Lao Tzu and Chuang Tzu in China and Shakyamuni Buddha in India are outstanding examples of this superb evolutionary breakthrough. Their teachings have a freshness and inspiration that assist humankind mightily even today. We can again see that the pattern of evolutionary advancement holds true here. The saints of our fourth stage can and have advanced three levels up to the seventh stage of true transcendence.

The Law of Contraction—Expansion

Before taking up a consideration of what lies ahead on the evolutionary path we can pause to make an important

reflection on the actual process of consciousness development exemplified both in those stages we have already
outlined and in the stages still to be envisaged. This process
is truly a matter of growth. Human awareness of what we
are and what everything is is growing. It is a process of
slowly awakening to what is actually going on. It is to be
stressed that this growth in awareness proceeds in two
seemingly opposite directions. Amazingly enough, the
more humans develop a greater and sharper identification
of individual beings, the more the consciousness expands
to awareness of the infinite. Tennyson, speaking of his own
experience, says: "All at once, as it were out of the intensity of the consciousness of individuality, individuality
itself seemed to dissolve and fade away into boundless
being . . ."[1] The more we become truly conscious of the
relative, the greater awareness we have of the absolute.
This is another way of saying that to become more awake
to what is is to eventually grow in consciousness of "both"
of the actual principles of being, form and formlessness.

Again, remember that these principles are not two
things. Since the beginning of western philosophical en-
deavor, the crucial problem has been that of the one and
the many. How can everything seem to be actually one
while at the same time it is obviously many things? Some
philosophers ultimately seem to deny the one, others the
many. But true growth of consciousness is a contraction to
fully experience the uniqueness of each one of the many
and in that very experience one's awareness expands to the
all-embracing, underlying oneness. We cannot help quoting the *Heart Sutra* once again: "Forms, these are the void.
The void, this is the forms." We must also repeat that these
two principles of being, which are also the two poles of
consciousness growth, are not existentially two. They are
not at all like the one atom of oxygen and two atoms of

hydrogen that form the two elements of one atom of water. In water we have two things becoming one (third) thing. The oneness that the many form beings share is not that of becoming a new thing, but that of simply being infinite potential in manifestation. This is not a numerical oneness, but the eternal flow (*tao*) of life manifesting in a myriad of forms. When we come to actually experience the reality of anything, our awareness is both contracting to see this unique mathematically one being and expanding to rejoice in the infinite *yin*/formlessness. This is spirit consciousness. This is reality.

The Advanced Stages

It is the history of culture, religion and language, in fact, the whole multifaceted history of the human race that reveals to us the four major stages of human consciousness evolution up to our present mental–egoic stage. At the same time these stages are known to us from reflection on our own personal histories from infancy up to now and from observation of other humans around us. In looking toward the future stages of consciousness evolution the question naturally arises as to what sources there are that can indicate future development with at least some degree of reliability. Again, both general history and to a lesser degree personal experience can adequately reveal the future of our race. As Wilber points out, there have been extraordinary persons in all ages whose consciousness has moved far in advance of that of their contemporaries. They are extraordinary precisely because they moved beyond the ordinary level of contemporary awareness up to as much as three levels above their own times.

Psychic Stage

Do this "to walk in the spirit"?

The fifth stage is that of psychic consciousness, which is dominated by the psyche or soul. As we have seen the various stages are differentiated according to that which dominates consciousness as a human processes his/her life experiences. At the first level the individual body awareness dominates; in the second, humans are somewhat free from their bodies and their imagination controls their lives. In the third it is group consciousness, and in the fourth it is mind. Here in the fifth stage the soul or psychic powers break free of the limitations of space, time and the ego, which have been established by the mind. For example, it is psychic when a mother knows even ahead of time about the injury of one of her children, often from a great distance. In such experiences it is clear that time and space are beginning to be transcended. Again, the ordinary "laws" of matter and energy discovered by fourth stage perception and intellection simply break down when a person walks on burning coals without the slightest pain or injury. They are also transcended when a person is psychically healed.

We can envisage this stage of development as ushering in an age in which psychic intuition is supreme. Economic, political and personal decisions will come to be made on intuition as well as rationality. Education will be a discipline geared toward more and more transcendence and immanence. This level of consciousness has been appearing in human society ever since the shamans of the second (magic) stage beginning roughly 200,000 years ago. Gradually it should come to hold sway generally.

T: I recall a Japanese lady who was with us at one of the first Zen retreats that I attended. After the retreat, when speaking about her *kensho* (basic enlightenment experience), she said that as her awareness deepened she came to see each of the pebbles in the garden beside the Zen hall with wonderful clarity. The uniqueness of each pebble stood out forcibly for her and yet they were all there in a shining, marvelous harmony and oneness. This, too, at least was psychic awareness and it manifests clearly the contraction–expansion process spoken of above.

When seated in deep meditation people will sometimes feel their bodies as very light and free. In fact, body energy can change so much that levitation can occur. The feeling about time can shift and thirty minutes can seem like five or ten. All such experiences are psychic. They are healthy signs of progress, but a person should resist the temptation to stop at only this advancement.

Archetypical Stage

As we proceed up the mountain of true awareness the next stage is that of devic or angelic consciousness. The word devic comes from the Sanskrit *deva*, a shining one. The Latin form is *deus* and the Greek *theos*, both of which, of course, mean god. Actually a much closer Judeo-Christian word for *deva* would seem to be angel. Here angel is not to be taken in its literal meaning of messenger, but as archetype. In the conception of reality we are following here, infinite potential (*yin*/formlessness/God) works its way down to individual manifestation through the causal forms we call archetypes. There are actual archetypes for humans, for male and female humans, for collie dogs, pine trees and quartz crystals. As a matter of fact, it is not unusual for a person in profound meditation to experience one breath to be every breath in existence. With such awareness the causal archetype is known in the perception of this individual act of being. This is termed devic, angelic, archetypical, causal consciousness. It is always accompanied by a sense of reverence and of returning to one's roots.

Anyone can dip into this awareness when wholeheartedly witnessing the expression of any action or quality. For example, you see a couple dancing a waltz with such grace, perfection and spirit that this waltz before your eyes somehow becomes every waltz that is ever danced. Tears come as you are overwhelmed with a rooted, expanded consciousness. For another example, say that you see a magnificent, totally unconditional act of compassion. Somehow you feel it to be compassion itself. In fact, you may say of the person so acting, "He/she is pure compassion!" Your consciousness can and does expand this way because this act is actually archetypical compassion in individual manifestation. You have become more aware of reality.

We have already noted that historically the pioneers of consciousness evolution have only been able to advance three levels above the general awareness of their times. This sixth level awareness is third level group consciousness advanced to its highest degree, to the archetype. Historically the various *dei* of ancient Roman mythology and the *theoi* of Greece have their origins in the period of the third stage. This pantheon of personified archetypes ranges from Pan and the nature gods, to Zeus and his consort Hera at the head of the hierarchy. In the east we see the same personification of the causal archetypes. In China archetypical compassion is represented as *Kuan Yin* (*Kannon* in Japanese) and millions are devoted to this "god." The highest fruit of such devotion is this sixth stage consciousness, which sees and is governed by compassion in everything. Some other devic "gods" still influential today in Japan, for example, are those of wisdom (*Fugen*), physical and emotional love (*Aizen*) and unwavering ascetical discipline (*Fudo*).

Archetypes reign over all time and space. Therefore, devic consciousness is characterized by great power. Actually giving oneself to this level demands a great loss of the narrow individually centered self. But this loss of self results in the actualization of self at the archetypical power level. Jesus of Nazareth is clearly presented in the gospels as operating at least at this level of consciousness. He consistently calls himself the "Son of Man." He thus identifies himself not merely as the son of Joseph (just as Peter is Simon, son of Jonah). He is archetypical. It would seem that it is the very power of the human archetype that he exercises when he easily heals other humans, since it is, of course, the power to produce healthy humans. "Power (archetypical human power) has gone out from me" (Lk 8:46).

Finally, it must be noted that since archetypes are still forms, devic consciousness is still a relational stage. Although it is an immensely expanded awareness, it is not formless, transrelational or truly transpersonal. There is still room for the personal self and some degree of subject–object separation in sixth stage consciousness. In religion the gods worshiped are personal and, historically speaking, are for the most part plural. However, the personification of archetypical power can be considered to have reached its final stage with the monotheism of Egypt and then of Israel.

In the west the first clearly monotheistic God emerged in Egypt in the time of King Iknaton (c. 1372–1354 B.C.). This God, Aton, is not just pre-eminent among many gods, but the only God, creator and source of all. Although the worship of Aton did not last in Egypt, the God revealed to Moses continued to dominate western culture up to this

very century. In the Mosaic religion Yahweh reigns everywhere, but remains ultimately the other, the independent
creator of heaven and earth. Humankind, working from a
state of separation, is ever seeking to rise to a beatific
relationship of union with this creator. All of this represents the highest level to which the sixth stage of consciousness can lead us.

Formlessness

Even in the highest degree of the sixth stage awareness
personal relationship remains. In the seventh and final
stage before the full integration called spirit consciousness
all of this relativity is lost. This seventh stage in our classification is actually the Great Death. It is the psychological
return to the infinite potential from which our existential
life emanates. Form (*yang*) recedes from the focus of
awareness and is superseded by formlessness (*yin*). In all
the six previous stages form has dominated. Now, in order
to come to the true balance of spirit consciousness, the
pendulum must swing for a time (probably only very
briefly) to the formless principle within all reality.

In Zen this change of awareness is called the "dropping off of mind and body." Our Zen master Yamada
Koun Roshi describes his own experience of this breakout
into infinity. In the afternoon of November 26, 1953 he
had been deeply struck by a saying of the great master
Dogen and was still under its influence when he awoke that
night about midnight. He repeated the saying to himself.

Then all at once I was struck as though by light-
ning, and the next instant *heaven and earth crum-
bled and disappeared.* Instantaneously, like surg-

ing waves, a tremendous delight welled up in me, a veritable hurricane of delight . . .[2] (Italics added)

The question at once arises as to whether this often brief experience can actually be called a *stage* of consciousness. Is it possible for a human being to remain for a long time without any awareness of form? The psychologically formless state would seem to be momentary or for some at most an ecstatic experience of an hour or two. However, in the case of the great modern Hindu Sri Ramana Maharshi and some others it seems to have gone on for long periods over many months. If all that one is aware of is nothingness, action in this relational world becomes impossible. In general, however, it would seem that the actual state is one in which consciousness is focused on the formless rather than consisting of a total non-perception of form. Of course, this focus is without deliberation or intention. It's as if in daily life one's awareness lens is literally focused on infinity rather than on one particular object. At any rate this consciousness is clearly presented as some kind of stage in the classic Zen account already quoted in Chapter 4, in which Wei-hsin no longer sees mountains or rivers. The same state is depicted in the eighth of the Oxherding Pictures, which outline the whole Zen path. The picture is of nothing but an empty circle and is titled: "Both Ox and Self Forgotten."

It is precisely in this movement into formlessness, and then on to the fullness of spirit consciousness, that we see the evolutionary advance of Jesus of Calvary over the Moses of Sinai. As already described in Chapter 7, Jesus in his life and above all in his Great Death experienced himself and all things as formless and beyond categories. It was through this death that he advanced to the goal of consciousness evolution, to risen life in the spirit. It was this Christ consciousness that overwhelmed the disciples during the Easter appearances and at Pentecost. It is this spirit consciousness that sees the formless Father in all forms and all forms in the formless—God in all and all in God. Jesus, the archetype of us all, says it clearly and powerfully in his fundamental statement, "I and the Father are one" (Jn 10:30).

This light is still at the deepest heart of Christianity, even though it must be admitted that the vast majority of Christians are still struggling with the problems of the mental-egoic stage. Some do advance now and then into the psychic and even devic stage. The integrating experience of transpersonal formlessness seems to be found only in some of the great mystics. However, at least some understanding of this literally crucial step does seem to be growing more widespread in our times. Christianity does seem to be making progress in discovering Christ Jesus as our evolutionary hero, as "the pioneer and perfecter of our faith" (Heb 12:2).

10. Life at the Summit

optional [um]"
Life in the Spirit
ie

Behold the birds of the air
and the lilies of the field.

—*Matthew 6*

A: I had completed my work at the University of California at Santa Barbara under Raymundo Pannikkar and was preparing to attend classes at the Graduate Theological Union, Berkeley. Fr. Hand had just returned from a trip to Japan and was telling about the retreats he had directed there and how he had been challenging people to express their actual purpose in life. He suddenly turned to me and asked me about my life's purpose. "What do you really want to be in life?" Without reflecting, I answered straight off, "A free and easy wanderer." This was a translation of the Chinese phrase *hsiao yao yu.* Some years before I had read this expression in *Chuang Tzu* and it echoed deep within me. I couldn't explain it well, but this verbalized my real ideal and deepest desire. By no means do I feel that I have come to the state of life-consciousness portrayed by these words, but if we are to seriously talk about life's purpose, our intention and motivation, I feel that this "free and easy wanderer" ideal must be presented and examined. It is not only the very heart of the philosophy of life taught by the easterners Chuang Tzu and Lao Tzu, it is also the true and highest spirit of the Christian gospel.

Free and easy wandering is actually the title of the first chapter of the seven that contain the heart of Chuang Tzu's philosophy of life. At the end of the last of these chapters,

133

he gives a striking exhortation to the highest spiritual way
of life.

> Do not be an embodier of fame; do not be a
> storehouse of schemes; do not be an undertaker of
> projects; do not be a proprietor of wisdom. *Embody to the fullest what has no end and wander
> where there is no trail.* (Italics added)[1]

From the first chapter to the last, Chuang Tzu tries by wild
words, paradoxical anecdotes, humor and reasoning to
shake us up and to convert us to a free, spontaneous, natural and joyful way of life—in a word, to the life of the
spirit. People of his time, just as of ours, were caught up in
a whole set of conventional values and limiting categories:
good and bad, true and false, ritually correct and incorrect,
like and dislike, reasonable and foolish, life and death,
time and space. In Chuang Tzu's view it is attachment to
these categories that ultimately causes us to suffer and to
make others suffer too. This suffering arises because attachment to all these conventional categories locks us into
a separate, exclusive self-identification. To preserve these
little egos we are possessed by fear, anxiety, aggression and
flight. Our life plans and projects are self-centered, full of
disharmony, tension and dis-ease. In place of all this,
Chuang Tzu urges us to plunge into the flow of tao. Literally, tao as a noun means way, and as a verb, speak. But for
now, without explaining further, we can take it to mean the
life force, the spirit. This force is the never ending movement from infinite potential to finite manifestation, from
formless to form. In the west this infinite potential is
termed God.

The way of life Chuang Tzu describes and urges us to

is a life that (1) embodies the spirit, and is (2) totally natural with a built-in orientation or purpose, (3) whose actualization is entered into through loss of the exclusive self, (4) resulting in a free and easy life of ineffable joy. This textbook-like enumeration is given to ensure clarity to this matter of ultimate importance.

Spirit Life

First, then, it is a life that is nothing but the manifestation of the infinite spirit. "Embody completely what has no limits" (chapter 7). In chapter six, Chuang Tzu personifies *tao,* using the terms creator and great ultimate teacher. In one place he has the enlightened sage Hsu Yu say:

> This teacher of mine, this teacher of mine, he
> passes judgment on the ten thousand things but
> he doesn't think himself righteous.
> His bounty extends to ten thousand generations
> but he doesn't think himself benevolent.
> He is older than the highest antiquity but he
> doesn't think himself long-lived.
> He covers heaven, bears up the earth, carves and
> fashions countless forms, but he doesn't think
> himself skilled.
> *It is with him alone I wander.* (Italics added)

This is clearly a picture of what westerners call God and life in God. Note, however, that Chuang Tzu by no means held this teacher to be an ontologically real person. We have already seen one phrase from a passage in the same chapter six, in which Chuang Tzu is describing the spirit life of two free and easy wanderers. Here is that phrase with more of the text:

Such men as they wander beyond the realm of phenomena. . . . Even now (in physical life) they have joined with the creator as men who wander in the single breath of heaven and earth . . . they wander free and easy in the work of self-less action.

Finally, in chapter seven, there is a remarkable passage in which a man named T'ien Ken (Heaven's Root) meets a nameless person! He asks him about how to rule the world. In his answer the nameless person seems to speak of moving on from a consciousness of relationship to a personified creator into the awareness that is totally in the non-categorical, infinite spirit flow. In such an interpretation the bird light-and-lissome will be the power of the spirit (the western dove) that seizes and elevates one's awareness during meditation.

The nameless man said, "Get away from me, you peasant! What kind of dreary question is that? I'm just about to set off with the creator. And if I get bored with that, then I'll ride on the light-and-lissome bird out beyond the six directions, wandering in the village of not-even-anything and living in the broad-and-borderless field. . . ."
But T'ien Ken repeated his question. The nameless man said, "Let your mind wander in simplicity, blend your spirit with the vastness, follow along with things the way they are, and make no room for personal views—then the world will be governed."

There are many more phrases Master Chuang uses to express the spiritual person (for example, "He takes his position in the immeasurable and wanders where there is nothing at all"—chapter 7), but using two phrases from the above quotation, we can move on to the other characteristics of life in the spirit.

The Way Things Are

The nameless person tells T'ien Ken to "follow along with things the way they are," or to follow the nature of things. The ideal life follows nature and its built-in orientation. The Chinese word for nature is *tzu jan*. *Tzu* means self, *jan* refers to suchness or so-ness. Chuang Tzu's phrase here, *wu tzu jan,* means "the suchness of things in themselves." Etymologically, the mysterious ideogram *jan* (such, so) is made of three parts: *yun* meaning uniform, even harmonious; *chuan,* dog, referring to animal life in general; and *huo,* fire, which traditionally suggests upward, advancing, brilliant movement. This etymology is by no means definitive, but the ideogram does suggest a living, harmonious movement. As the poet Gerard Manley Hopkins puts it, "There lives the dearest freshness deep down things." This is the dynamism of the spirit giving life and action to everything. This spirit is the ultimate nature of everything. We need but follow it.

T: The little story told me by a Japanese friend is apropos here. She and her husband had called in a man to give their garden a well needed trimming. He was a real professional and his work was rather expensive. When she saw him quite frequently stop, stand back, light up a cigarette and relax, she began to feel uneasy. Finally, she went to her husband and complained about how he was laying down on the job and not earning his pay. He laughed at her and told her she was foolish. "Don't you realize that he is just looking at the trees, listening for them to tell him where and how to cut?"

In fact, ideally, the creation of a Japanese garden is
wholly done in this organic way. This rock is put down and
it tells you whether it is sitting correctly, because every
rock has its own best way of sitting. Then, when this tree or
shrub is put by the rock, they both inform you whether or
not they belong together. A man in southern California,
who loved things Japanese, drew up some plans for a Japanese garden he wanted to build at his home. Finally, he
took the plans to a native Japanese gardener in the area.
The first thing the gardener said was, "Tear up the plans!"
One cannot help but contrast this viewpoint with that of
the mathematical designs imposed upon nature in the great
gardens of Kew and Versailles.

This brings us to take up those lines which we quoted,
but did not comment upon, found at the beginning of this
section. "Do not be an embodier of fame; do not be a
storehouse of schemes; do not be an undertaker of projects;
do not be a proprietor of wisdom." Why does Chuang Tzu
so disparage planning and projects, even wisdom and repu-
tation? The answer is that he does not trust the ego mind.
From his own experience he knows that we do not see the
suchness (the reality) either of things or of ourselves. We
mis-take the way things are. When we follow the ego mind,
we easily stray from the natural path of life. This ego mind
is constantly expressing its mistakes in our plans, projects
and clever wisdom.

This is why Chuang Tzu speaks about the true person
as one who "doesn't allow likes or dislikes to get in and do
him harm. He just lets things be the way they are (follow
their nature) and doesn't try to help life along" (chapter 5).
And again he recommends "not using the mind to repel the
tao, not using man (ego schemes) to help out heaven"
(chapter 6). Finally, in chapter 4, Master Chuang tells us
that "to know that-which-cannot-be-otherwise and to con-

tentedly take (it) as the order of nature is the perfection of
the actualization of *tao*" (authors' translation).

In these last three quotations there are three terms
which help us to understand Chuang Tzu's insight about
the natural life: order (*ming*); heaven (*t'ien*); and that-
which-cannot-be-otherwise (*pu te ui*). Our master certainly
experienced an order, a built-in orientation, in all nature.
This is order both in the sense of purposeful arrangement
and in the sense of command. The ideogram for this
"order" has as its first meaning simply life (*ming*)! So *life*
itself has a built-in *order* and *command*. Sometimes *ming*
is used with *t'ien* (heaven's order, command, or just
heaven alone). In the terminology we have been following,
heaven is the spirit or life-force. So strong is this "order"
that ultimately things "cannot-be-otherwise." The spirit,
the dynamism of nature, is actually ruling all things. Anyone who experiences being in this flow discovers that
things happen with a certain inevitability. In the process of
making decisions, a spirit person simply knows the way
that things must flow and follows along. This is a very deep
consciousness (or elevated, if you wish). People with advanced awareness down through the ages all come to this
sense of what Jesus of Nazareth called the reign of God.
Master Chuang had this consciousness preeminently. For
this reason he insistently calls for the loss of that scheming,
manipulating, self-centered ego that "repels the *tao*."

Face Lift

The final word of advice the nameless person gives is,
". . . make no room for personal views." A literal translation of the Chinese is: "Do not countenance the private."
We need to change our countenance. We must turn it upward, away from fixation on the self-centered ego. A face

lift is needed. We should not countenance the exclusively private but face up to the spirit that is discovered only in the all-inclusive self of enlightenment. The loss of the exclusively private self has already been amply discussed, especially in Chapters 2, 3 and 7. It is time, then, to consider the kind of activity such a loss allows to be born.

Chuang Tzu uses a highly revealing expression to describe the life and action of a spirit person. He says that a true person "does not act"; at least this is the usual translation of the two ideograms *wu* (not) and *wei* (act, do, make) which he uses here. However, the type of action *wei* refers to is *action for the sake of*. This use of the ideogram is especially true, it seems, in the time of Chuang Tzu. (Japanese took this ideogram from China, and in Japan it is used not only as the verb "act," but more frequently in prepositional phrases: "for the sake of, on behalf of, in order to"). So Master Chuang is insisting that the action of an enlightened person is "not action for the sake of." It is just action. There is no need for any purpose to be added on. Every action *by its nature* has a built-in orientation *to give life*. Where would this added on purpose come from? Only from the separated ego–mind! Instead of just "having coffee" in the morning, I have to "have *my* coffee." Instead of simply doing, I have to "do it *my* way." And what is to be said of the expression "My God"? A sense of the exclusive, separating self seems so strong in all this. It is the ego–mind that is the problem. As a Chinese fortune cookie had it once, "Life is what happens to you *while you are* busy making other plans."

The enlightened mind, because it knows the spirit that enlivens all things, knows what things are in themselves (*tzu jan*) and feels the intrinsic orientation of the spirit within. It is "original sin" thinking and willing that, "like a God," sets up a separate world with its added on purposes.

And when is this purpose added on? When we try to plan, decide and act without enlightenment. The following texts of both Chuang Tzu and Lao Tzu must be seen within the context of their societies, in which the ruler played such an overwhelming role. Both of the philosophers put their ideas to practical application in the vital matter of the ideal ruler. In such passages, of course, we can learn much not just about a ruler but also about the ideal human being in general.

In a few brilliant lines Lao Tzu describes both the true and the lower type ruler. The true is so enlightened by the mystery of the spirit that he is inarticulate and only mumbles "is *mun mun*." He is so aware of the nature of people that he lets them act according to their simple reality. But the lower level ruler is sharp and discriminating in his own clever wisdom.

> When the ruler is mun, mun,
>   the people are simple, simple.
> When the ruler is sharp, sharp,
>   the people are discontented, discontented.

> —*Tao Te Ching, chapter 58*

Chuang Tzu is just as eloquent:

> Chien Wu said, "He (Chung Shih) told me that the ruler of men should devise his own principles, standards, ceremonies, and regulations, and then there will be no one who will fail to obey him and be transformed by them."
>
> The madman Chieh Yu said, "This is bogus virtue (false actualization of the flow)! To try to govern the world like this is like trying to walk the

ocean, to drill through a river, or to make a mosquito shoulder a mountain! When the sage governs, does he govern what is on the *outside?* He makes sure of himself first, and then he acts. He makes absolutely certain that things can do what they are supposed to do, that is all" (chapter 7).

Contrast the Lao–Chuang way of planning and acting with the interminable meetings, the tortured working out of goals and means, the detailed laws and regulations so prevalent in our organizations. Think, also, of the need to stroke the egos of everyone, the image making, the public relations campaigns and all the other machinations of our struggling ego consciousness. We are far from the spirit ideal, but it is important to acknowledge it as *our* ideal, as the state to which we are destined to advance.

There are two common, practical objections to this way of life. One, that it's too passive, and, two, that it's out of this real world. However, this advanced state of living is by no means a passivity in which we allow others and/or circumstances of life to make all our decisions and rule our lives. On the contrary, it is the supreme degree of responsibility. In it we know existentially that the spirit is actually ruling every event. In the TV mini-series, *Out on a Limb,* when David and Shirley are standing on the side of a canyon looking down to where a whole busload of people had died, David quietly affirms that there is a higher harmony at work in everything, that excessive grief over death and especially rebellion against it is shortsighted. Enlightenment does not lead to passivity but to a state beyond the distinction of active and passive, to a life filled with the dynamism of this harmony. One simply moves in/as the flow.

I am

It must be noted that all this does not mean that there will be no reports and planning and consideration of practical steps. But data gathering will be for the discovery of the true nature of things. Meetings will be filled with the discernment of spirits with strict guard against the intrusion of the narrow ego spirit. For it all to work there must be some level of enlightenment. Without this we just have to muddle along as best as we can and suffer the consequences. This suffering, too, is the spirit at work!

As to the objection that this ideal is impractical and out of the real world, it all depends, of course, upon what you consider the real world. Is an egocentric world real? Yes, it does have a certain relative reality. But more basically it is an illusion, a mis-take. People who make this objection, though, usually mean real as indicating the world of competing egos, of manipulating bosses at the office, of using all one's time to care for a sick child, of struggling to put food on the table, of fear in the cities, of child abuse, alcoholism, drugs and gnawing wars—cold and hot. The "real world" is not pretty. It is anxiety, fear, insecurity, hard work and struggle. So strong and blinding is this spirit that if a man goes walking down the street with a bounce, a big grin and a song, many people will turn, look back at him and say, "Hey, what's wrong with him?" The spirit person truly sees this very real world, but his/her consciousness advances deep within to find the spirit, the reign of God, in everything. The true person feels the pain and the glory at the same time, both the disharmony and the higher harmony ever at work.

Finally, an advanced consciousness is eminently practical. It does work and it creates true happiness. Witness the lasting effects of the non-violence movement of the Mahatma, Gandhi. Which is a more practical and basically

more efficient way to plan and take a course of action: to
stand apart and judge whether things fit *my* purpose (or the
purpose of our company, our family, our religion or nation), then to act for my (our) sake, or to sense the inner
nature of the people, events, action in question, then to
follow their nature and their built-in orientation? A course
of planning and action is practical and real if it leads certainly to the actualization of our *true* goals. It is eminently
practical, then, to discern and follow the spirit, not the
unreal, self-defeating self.

Joie de Vivre

From a college paper in Japan:

When I was in the last year of primary school, I
belonged to the track and field club. I didn't like
sports, but my homeroom teacher forced me to
join the club. It was very hard. Even during summer vacation it continued and all of us were
always sweating. After vacation we had an even
harder exercise. I thought only of a way to escape.

One day we checked our records. We all had
to run 100 meters and to record the time. When
my turn came I was very nervous. "On your
mark!" "Set!" "Go!" *I didn't think* of anything.
My hands and legs moved *by themselves*. I kicked
the ground with my feet and the wind took after
me. At this moment I felt all things; the sky, wind,
ground, and the others surrounding me were only
one with me. But I don't mean that things were a
part of me, but I was a part of things.

That's my first experience. It was a very special feeling, as if I had been melting *into nature*.

And it was an easy feeling. I kept *running at ease.*
It is too difficult to express that experience. My
record was the best time I'd ever run.

Now I am too fat and older. Even if I wish to
run like that, I can't do it anymore. But when I try
to run as fast as possible, I can still feel something
of that time. It's like a *peace of mind.* I feel that I
am included in something very wide.

This little story from the account of a Japanese college
student brings us to the final point of our presentation of
the human ideal of classical Taoism. In her brief experience Inaba Hiromi San just dipped into true consciousness
for a short while and her running became free and easy. No
effort, just free action. As Master Chuang so eloquently
assures us, when we get to the summit there is freedom and
joy. A person burdened with an unenlightened, exclusive
self as the motivating force behind all his/her activities in
life is always struggling. Fear of failure and ambition for
success make such a person a slave. Actions built on judgments of like and dislike, good and bad, can be unbeliev-
ably painful when what is bad or disliked cannot be
avoided. The pressure of one's *own* goals and "dead"-lines
can drive a person to drink. And the guilt of drink and
other escapes can end in self-destruction. There is no limit
to the burdensome labor and trouble that false self-awareness can bring.

In contrast to all this Chuang Tzu presents the ideal
person as one who goes through life happily playing (*yu*)!
Once the illusion of the exclusive self has lifted, life becomes like a profoundly joyful game. The full expression is
hsiao yao yu: hsiao, to move leisurely; *yao,* removed (from
the demands of false self-awareness); *yu,* to travel freely, to
play. The picture is of a person who experiences life as

nothing but a manifestation of the free, dynamic, creative flow, ever ancient, ever new. Such a person works, naturally, but never labors. Purpose, strength, skillful means, security, companionship, everything that is needed and more is inexhaustibly found in the world of spirit manifesting. Moving with the unceasing ebb and flow of the formative, then the transformative action of the life force, the true person enjoys life as a child losing self in the delights of playing.

In conclusion, Master Chuang speaks to us directly:

> You have had the audacity to take on human
>   form
>   and you are delighted.
> But the human form has ten thousand changes
>   that never come to an end.
> Your joys, then, must be uncountable.
> Therefore the sage wanders in the realm
>   where things cannot get away from him
>   and all are preserved.
> He delights in early death; he delights in old age.
> He delights in the beginning; he delights in the
>   end.
> If he can serve as a model of men,
>   how much more so THAT,
>   which the ten thousand things are tied to
>   and all changes alike wait upon.

—Chapter 6

11. One, Two, Three—
Ten Thousand

We ten thousand things dance
and enjoy life together
in the one breath of heaven and earth.

—Oliver Owl Form

A: Years ago, I think it was in the early 1970s, there was a movie with the very strange Chinese title: *Animals' Bisexuality.* However, its brief newspaper introduction somehow evoked my interest and intuitively I felt that there was something to be learned from it, so I went. The movie was a British production, a documentary on the evolution of life from the very beginning of the evolutionary process. It went from a one cell creature up the scale of formation and through the entire process of birth–aging–decaying–death–then life again. The whole film was well done and very impressive. One scene which I can't forget even up to this day, was about the death of a rabbit. The camera with its slow motion showed the whole decomposition process of the dead rabbit beginning with the eyes. Gradually, gradually we saw the disappearance of the rabbit form (body) until there was nothing left. Then, instantaneously, from the very spot where the rabbit passed on, out came a plant and then a flower. I was very much enraptured by this scene and somehow glimpsed the mystery of life itself. I began to ask myself, "What is that which is beyond the rabbit form and plant form and flower form and even my human body form? How are all of these

147

forms related? Where do forms come from and where do they go?"

God-Talk/Life-Talk

In our first chapter we stated one of the underlying themes of this book by saying that God is different. In this chapter we want to conclude our presentation of this theme by offering another, even broader statement: "Life is different." The questions raised at the end of the rabbit story above are questions about life. It is in the context of the most fundamental questions about life that we wish to approach the mystery which we call God. We will do this from the far eastern viewpoint. This chapter, then, is about God, especially God as personal, as triune and as incarnate.

Strictly speaking, China and the far east do not have any such God-talk. They simply have "life-talk." No theology as such ever developed in the far east, only philosophy of life; and life is seen as one dynamic, ever changing flow. When things move they are alive. When they don't move they are dead. The great Chinese book *I Ching* is probably the oldest book in the world. The title means "A Treatise (*Ching*) on Change (*I*)" or "A Treatise on the Flow." We are convinced that it will be most helpful to look at the great Christian teachings about God (as personal, triune, incarnate) using the light of the most ancient Chinese philosophy of life. We will take this philosophy from classical Taoist sources with some influence from Mahayana Buddhism.

For Christians only one thing is necessary: to know and to enter into the Christ experience. The original inner experience of Jesus and his first disciples is the only thing that is essential to Christianity. All else—scriptures, dogmas, sacraments, liturgies, etc.—are only skillful means to this end. We are Christians to the degree that we share this experience. Ultimately, it can never be defined, because one element of the experience is formless, infinite, indefinable. The descriptions of this experience given by Jesus, by the primitive church and by all ages of the Christian church up until recent times have all been from within the mental framework of the western consciousness, especially the Judeo-Greco-Roman worldview. The credal formulas carefully worked out mainly during the first five centuries of church history are basically western expressions of the Christ experience. Down through the ages they have been of immense assistance to the faithful along the Christian path, especially when they have been used *without attachment*. But they are inescapably western in concepts and words.

The point of all this is that, speaking from our own experience, we feel that it is eminently true to say that insights and expressions from *outside* the Mediterranean world can help Christians very much to discover the original inner experience of Jesus and his disciples. At the same time they can assist us immensely to create an expression of the Christ experience that will be more helpful to Christians both east and west.

However, before presenting the Chinese philosophical expression of the experience of life, we will briefly outline the Christian. Seeing the two together will highlight not only the similarities, but especially the differences. It is in the differences that enrichment and enlightenment can occur, if we are open.

We Believe in One God . . .

The Hebrew roots of Christianity represent God as one, as Yahweh. In the patriarchal Hebrew society this

God is given a male gender. Jesus certainly experienced God as one, yet there are three spoken of in the New Testament that in some way or another share in divinity. The trinitarian formulas about God which reached their full development by the fourth century are by no means clearly and unequivocably taught in the New Testament. In this respect, the trinitarian formulas of the church fathers represent a development of doctrine.

God is defined as three persons: Father, Son and Spirit, although the concept of person is not to be taken with all the meaning given it in modern times. The three persons are distinct but related because they all share the one, unique divine nature. They are only one God. God is distinct from and totally independent of creation. On the other hand, humans are destined to somehow share in the eternal divine life and all creatures are manifestations of the triune God in some way. Jesus of Nazareth is the Son of God incarnate. He, as one person, possesses both a divine and human nature. Through Jesus and in him, especially through his sacrificial death and his resurrection, it is possible for all humans to enter into union with God in eternal life. This is salvation. Perhaps many nuances and refinements should be added to this outline of Christian theology of life. Having made this statement, we leave it to our readers to add whatever they might deem necessary.

The Taoist Trinity

Just as in Christian theology, so in Chinese philosophy, life is ultimately trinitarian. The earliest Chinese philosophers were Taoist, and the two greatest of these were Lao Tzu and Chuang Tzu. We will be using the *Tao Te Ching* of Lao Tzu as our main source in this discussion. The title of his short and only extant work is perhaps best translated as "A Treatise on the Actualization of the Life Flow" (*tao* is life flow, *te* is actualization, *ching* is treatise). The trinitarian aspect of the Chinese philosophy of life pervades all of Chinese thought and culture even to this day. The number of human beings that have lived according to the basic assumptions of this philosophy certainly outnumbers the Christian groups and probably all other populations in history. But it is more for its intrinsic superlative excellence that it deserves our open-minded attention.

The basic trinitarian aspect of life, of absolutely everything, is beautifully capsulized in the forty-second chapter of the *Tao Te Ching:*

> *Tao* gives birth to one.
> One gives birth to two.
> Two gives birth to three.
> Three gives birth to the ten thousand things.
> The ten thousand things carry *yin* and embrace
>   *yang.*
> Filled with the vital force they act in harmony.

Tao, dynamic reality, is literally translated as "way." This indicates something like way in the expression, "He cut his way through the crowded room." *Tao* means being. But being has come to have a very static connotation in English, so it would be better to say *is-ing*. Most of the time we will leave the Chinese word untranslated, *tao,* but remember to read it as dynamic be-ing, is-ing or life.

To understand the above passage we best start with the last two sentences. First, "The ten thousand things carry *yin* and embrace *yang*." The ten thousand things means all the things that exist. Things here means all actual forms of any kind from the most dense of physical bodies to the thinnest of thought forms. Everything that is in a form of any kind is changeable. First it starts to appear. It grows to full manifestation. Then as soon as it is fully grown, it starts to decline and ultimately disappears into that infinite potential which appeared as this particular form in the first place. But this very disappearance is the beginning of the next form. So the movement goes on and on in a cyclic way, formless to form to formless to . . . As Lao Tzu, in chapter 40, says, "The movement of tao is cyclic." The ten thousand things are said to "carry *yin*" because we carry things on our backs. *Yin* is that which is the "back of" all forms. It is that which cannot be seen. It is formless. Everything is said to "embrace *yang*," because what we embrace is in front and can be seen. *Yang* is form.

Yin and *yang*, formless and form, are "filled with the vital force" (*ch'i* in Chinese; *ki* in Japanese). It is this life force that moves *yin*, formless, to manifest as forms, and *yang* to return to formlessness. So the constitution of everything is a trinity: *yin—yang—*movement, and these three are one. "They act in harmony." When things are open and put no impediments to the free movement of the vital force, everything is harmony, peace and happiness. This is the Chinese philosophy of life.

One, Two, Three—Ten Thousand

Given the trinity of formless, form and their vital movement, we can look at the first four verses of chapter 42. "Tao gives birth to one." To "give birth to" here simply indicates what comes forth when one existentially looks at be-ing (tao). Looking at any and all be-ings, the first thing we see is form. Everything has some form. In fact, the Chinese word Lao Tzu uses for form be-ing is *yu*, which means *having* (form). In the order of discovery this

is the first of the three principles we find when we analyze
life. Form is number "one." So what is left to see in our
analysis? Nothing. Yes, that which next comes up in Lao
Tzu's analysis is no-thing. All forms appear and then disappear. They come into form and then go to formless. The
Chinese word is *wu yu* (*no* form) or simply *wu* (form*less*).
Add this to form and we have "two." Looking at life as
these two we also see that they are always moving. There is
constant movement from form to formless to form to
formless to . . . We have already *yin* as a name for the
formless and *yang* for form. Thus, as we concluded before,
be-ing is the trinity of *yin*–*yang*–movement. These "three
give birth to the ten thousand things."

This *yin*–*yang*–*ch'i* movement is traditionally expressed in the superbly worked out *t'ai chi* (supreme ultimate) diagram.

Being is flowing in a circle. *Yang* (form) is above in white,
because white is all colors in one. *Yin* (formless) is below in
black, absence of all color. Starting at the bottom is formless *yin,* which rises up only to appear as form. Form develops to a fullness and then falls back down into formlessness. This movement goes on and on and is indicated
by the wavy line. This wavy line, which is joined together
with the circle line, shows that *yin* and *yang* are existentially one. A straight line would seem to cut them into two
halves. This same existential oneness is indicated by the
dot of *yin* right within *yang* and vice versa. *Yin* is always
spoken of first because formlessness is the source of form.
Finally, we want to insist that this diagram and the analysis
of life it represents is all just an expression of the actual

experience of the early Taoist philosopher mystics. They truly saw into life and described it as be-ing in three principles. This *yin–yang–ch'i* paradigm is all pervasive in Chinese philosophy, medicine, politics, and general culture even to this day.

God in Life-Talk?

We can arrive at a better understanding of this dynamic philosophy of life by comparing it with the familiar Christian paradigm. To begin with there is no personal God in the strict sense. There are only three principles of life. Nor is there a God that is independent from all the ten thousand things (all creation). The formless is mysterious and infinite, but is never apart from the myriad of forms it appears in. In fact, formless and form are mutually interdependent, not just conceptually, but existentially in life. From his own experiences, Lao Tzu puts all this succinctly in chapter 25.

> There is something undefined, complete,
> born before heaven and earth.
> How silent! How boundless!
> It stands alone, unchanging,
> pervading all unceasingly.
> One may call it mother of the world.
> I do not know its name.
> As a pseudonym I say *tao*.
> If I have to give it a name,
> I shall say "big".
> Big means going on and on.
> Going on and on means returning.

"Something undefined, complete, born before heaven and earth" is certainly the experience of the infinite, perfect be-ing Christians call God. The phrase "born before" is just a way of saying that the whole universe of form proceeds from this "something," which is not a thing, because, strictly speaking, it has no "name."

"It stands alone, unchanging, pervading all unceasingly." This sentence is of greatest importance. This "something" stands alone not in the sense that it is ever apart from forms. Rather it pervades all. But it is different from all forms because all forms change whereas it is unchanging, unceasing. There truly are two principles being spoken of, but they are mutually interdependent. Forms arise from the formless and are always nothing but this "something" in manifestation. On the other hand, the formless does not "exist," i.e. stand out, except in forms. Lao Tzu declares this mutual interdependence in chapter 2, when he says: "Form (*yu*) and formless (*wu*) give birth to one another." It is precisely this interdependence that preserves the intrinsic oneness of all be-ing. The flow from formless to form to formless to . . . is only one life movement at the same time as it is a true multiplicity of forms changing.

We can note here that the fact that all life is only one formless-form flow is at the root of the "both-yes-and-no-talk" common to all who have truly experienced life. Yes, this "something" *is* formless. No, it does not *exist* except as forms. Yes, it is unchanging. No, it is always changing as forms. Yes, it is alone. No, it is pervading all. This kind of talk arises because this "something" is not a thing. It is not in any category, yet it flows in all categories, even contradictory ones. It transcends all, yet it is totally one with all.

The consciousness of life as one formless-form flow can be called *full consciousness*. It does see the formless principle as distinct from form, but as existentially one in the one flow of life. To see anything, especially one's self, as only form is a mis-take which we can call *incomplete consciousness*. It is from this kind of consciousness that "either-yes-or-no-talk" proceeds. This distinguishes only the multiplicity of everything and can never grasp either the formless or the oneness of the many in the formless. This consciousness is actually only darkness passing as light. It is still very common in modern theology and philosophy.

Father/Mother God

"One may call it the mother of the world." We have already mentioned that this infinite "something" is not strictly personal in Taoism, because that would put it into a definite category. However, for practical reasons, both Lao Tzu and Chuang Tzu do personify it to some degree. Chuang Tzu calls this unnameable principle master, teacher, creator. Lao Tzu uses many symbols (storehouse, treasure, uncarved block), but only one real personification, that of mother. One is tempted to see in this personification a carry over from the Great Goddess of the third stage of consciousness evolution. Of course, Lao Tzu himself, like ourselves, is of the fourth stage (which begins around 2000 B.C.) but far closer to the third than we are.

In third stage thought life comes from the feminine. The male part of procreation is hardly understood. Babies come from mothers in birth, so the life principle itself was personified as the Great Mother and worshiped as the Great Goddess. It is easy to imagine how this imagery would carry over into a philosophy of life like Taoism. It is interesting to note that one of the two ideograms used in

Buddhism to express this infinite principle is graphically
feminine. The first ideogram 空, emptiness, expresses the
principle as formless. The second, 如, pictures the "suchness" of everything, that infinite something which manifests itself in every form being. 女 means woman, and 口
is an opening. An unmistakable graphic of the "mother of
the world."

Continuing along this vein, it is worth noting that only
in the fourth stage of evolution does masculine personification take over. The male God is most often seen as the all
powerful ruler of all. A male God, by himself, without a
female consort, is not so much life-giver, but a power figure, a Lord. It was within this mental framework that Jesus
had to express his experience. Jewish religion was centered
around the Lord God. Humans had to follow his will,
commandments and reign. Life was a matter of keeping a
covenant with God who judged the actions of all, giving
rewards and punishments. Jesus took this masculine Lord
God and presented him as *Abba,* a loving father. But still
the authority/power mentality remains. After Jesus "goes
to the Father" and is "seated at his right hand (of power)"
he is declared Lord with "all authority in heaven and on
earth." In Taoist terms Jesus would have said "I go to the
Mother" in order to indicate his definitive death to all
forms through bodily death and his rising to the fullness of
creative *life.* Of course this "life" theme is also found in the
Bible, especially in John's gospel.

As to the whole question of a personal God we feel that
Lao Tzu and Chuang Tzu would simply consider personalizing the infinite principle as a means to assist people on
the way. We have already spoken along this line in earlier
chapters of this book. There and here we are looking at the
whole matter from a Taoist/Mahayana consciousness
without making any claims as to the correctness or validity

of this consciousness. Personalizing the absolute principle
of life is for Lao–Chuang something to be used freely without any attachment. We humans are usually struggling
along the path with an immensely strong sense of our relational self. We literally find and constitute ourselves, both
as individuals and as identified with a group, in relationships with others. Having such a self-consciousness,
humans almost inevitably make the formless, infinite principle of life into a somebody to whom we can relate. This
projected relationship is most helpful and strength-giving
as we face the difficulties and sufferings that threaten the
development, happiness, even continued existence of our
selves. But personification is ultimately only helpful if it is
used without attachment. Lao–Chuang warns us not to
absolutize any relationship. The great danger here is to
continue to the end in seeing the formless principle as an
other to whom we as persons relate. If it is other to us, we
can never find ourselves as that very principle. We can
never experience our true life. We are nothing but the
formless in human forms. We must be able to say both,
"Yes, I am formless," and "Yes, I am form," because this
is the very constitution of human life. "To go to the Father
(Mother)" is to enter this *full consciousness.* As the basic
condition of following him, Jesus demands that we deny
and lose our "this form only" self. There is no other way to
the fullness of life.

Still considering the matter of the personal infinite, we
feel that Lao–Chuang would be very interested in the original meaning of hypostasis, the term used by the Greek
church fathers to describe each "person" of the Trinity.
The modern idea of person is an intelligent, separate subject related to all the many other beings. This they would
certainly reject as unsuitable to apply to the unlimited
principle of life. However, the word hypostasis means

something that stands (*stasis*) under (*hypo*). Since the "three that stand under" in the Christian Trinity in no way destroy the actual oneness of God, the term hypostasis seems to be a good one to apply as well to the Taoist trinity of *yin, yang,* and *ch'i.* Of course, one must keep in mind that in the Christian paradigm the three hypostases are only in the divinity, whereas in taoism they refer to the three principles of life in all its forms.

Finally, we can note that in the actual practice of Chinese religions there is a great amount of personal relationship and devotion. First, there are personifications of special manifestations of the infinite life principle in such popular objects of devotion as *Kuan Yin* (compassion) and *Amida* (light and salvation). Then there is the "quasi-deification" of the great historical figures who were special manifestations of life during their time on earth and are now objects of devotion and earnest petitionary prayer. The greatest example of this is Buddha himself. Whether *Kuan Yin* and *Amida* were ever actual historical persons is not certain. Lastly, there is the devotion paid to family ancestors as special representatives of the family's spirit and source of its present life. The reason for saying all this is to point out that there is ample fulfillment in Chinese and other far eastern cultures of the ingrained human need for personal, religious devotion.

Lao–Chuang and Jesus

In the Christianity of the Nicene Creed, Jesus of Nazareth is held to be one divine person (hypostasis) who possesses two natures, human and divine. This union of humanity and God in the one person is termed hypostatic. This is the ultimate solution given to the problem of uniting humankind with God. This very Christian problem arises because of the great distinction made between God and creatures. God is infinite and humanity is finite. Humankind is always dependent upon God but God is always independent of us. By sin, humankind effectively denies its dependence upon God. The God made flesh Jesus came both to unite the infinite and the finite in his own person and to reestablish humankind in its dependence upon God. Jesus is our mediator with God. He is our high priest or pontifex (bridge maker). Through his being and actions as God made flesh, all humanity is saved. We are saved by entrusting ourselves to him.

Neither in Taoism nor in Buddhism is there an existential distinction between formless (God) and form (creation). They are interdependent principles joined in the one flow of life. Both Lao Tzu and Chuang Tzu would say to each of us Christians, "You are just as much the child of God as Jesus of Nazareth is, with the great difference that he experiences himself as such and you are not yet fully in that state of awareness. There is no separation or distinction between your full self and what you call God. Your salvation consists in dying to your *incomplete consciousness* of self and in discovering that you are the infinite no-thing from which your human form and all the ten thousand things arise. This is eternal life. Jesus is there and can lead you to it. Follow him. Discover with him and rejoice!"

Some of Lao Tzu's own words on all of this, which can very well be read as the words of the crucified, risen Jesus Christ, are:

Entering into utmost emptiness
I maintain the stillness wholeheartedly.
All things are moving together,

Thus I contemplate their cyclic movement.
So many, many things!
Each returns to the source.
Returning to the source is called silence.
Silence is called the return to life.
Returning to life is called the eternal state.
To know the eternal is enlightenment.
When one does not know the eternal,
blindness causes disaster.
Knowing the eternal, one becomes one with all.
Being one with all, one is without attachment.
Being without attachment, one becomes ruler.
Becoming ruler one becomes divine.
Becoming divine one becomes the flow of life.
Becoming the flow of life one becomes
     imperishable.
and even the dissolution of the body is not
     destruction.

—Chapter 16

All that we have presented here in this tenth chapter
may have been rather difficult reading at times, so we
would like to end with a little fantasy which we composed.
In it we are simply summing up many of the themes of the
chapter. (So that you can pronounce the title as it is intended, please note that the "T" in Taoist is more correctly
enunciated as a "D".)

A Taoist Dialogue

A turtle and an owl are traveling the same path. The
owl is quietly resting on a low branch enjoying the wonderful view. The turtle comes puffing up.

Turtle: Who are you? What are you called?

Owl: I am formless.

T.: Oh, I'm called formless, too. Are we the same thing?

O.: No, we are two things.

T.: But you are formless and so am I. It seems like we are one.

O.: Oh, this time you are right. We are one.

T.: How confusing. We are two, but yet we are one thing.

O.: Whoops! There you go again. One is not a thing. It seems that you have not been brought up very well. Tell me your name.

T.: Well, it's rather long and quite confusing. But my name is Isaac T.F. Formless. The T.F. stands for Turtle Form. What's your name?

O.: I am Oliver Owl Form. The formless part is not really a name. Didn't anyone ever tell you that?

T.: No. Is that why we can be forms and formless at the same time?

O.: Fine. We are simply two as forms and one as formless.

T.: This is *very* enlightening. I never even knew who I was before! Or who anybody is, either. May I ask you another question? Where are you going?

O.: No where.

T.: But you look like you really are moving to somewhere. Let's just stroll along together. I, too, am going nowhere in particular.

O.: I didn't say nowhere. I said no where. You are really mixed up, aren't you?

T.: Mixed up! You're the one who's mixed up. No-where is nowhere and . . .

O.: Just a minute. Let me ask you a question. Where are you from?

T.: Well, to be honest, I really don't know, so I always just say nowhere. It's all so scary. I feel like I'm just going around in circles.

O.: Very good. Our movement is circular. But don't mix up nowhere with no where.

T.: This is beginning to sound like your talk about formless being no thing.

O.: Excellent! Yes, no where and no thing are identical. Your complexion is beginning to change. How do you feel?

T.: I'm beginning to feel very light.

O.: You mean both not-heavy-light and not-dark-light?

T.: Yes. That's it! And I just realized that not just you and I, but the ten thousand things are actually ten thousand and one. I am one of the things and one with everything.

O.: Yes! So at last you are saved from all those mistakes and fears. Now you know.

T.: Wonderful. I have never thought of such a thing.

O.: Right again. The suchness of things is not something you can think about.

T.: I'm full of life and feel so light I'm dancing.

O.: Yes. Yes. This is Life. We ten thousand beings dance and enjoy life together in the one breath of heaven and earth.

12. Esoteric Reading

> Unless you find paradise
> at your own center,
> there is not the smallest chance
> that you may enter.

> —*Angelus Silesius*

A: Christianity is generally recognized as a religion of the word. The Bible as the word of God is central to Christian life. Even before I became a Christian I had an experience of this fact. I remember vividly how impressed and moved I was by certain words of the New Testament. It was during my first year of senior high school. One of my classmates was the daughter of a Presbyterian minister. She had the habit of reading scripture at school right in the midst of non-Christians. She did this practice before her lunch. For a long time I watched her and was very much attracted to her practice, even to the point of feeling envious of her privilege. Secretly I wished that some day I would have the same privilege as she did. One day as she was quietly reading to herself, I stretched my ears to listen to her words.

> Blessed are the poor in spirit . . .
> Blessed are the meek . . .
> Blessed are the pure of heart, for they shall see
>   God.

This last sentence not only has stayed with me ever since I heard my classmate read it, but has also drawn me deeper into its spirit and life. Actually, I was not sure that I understood the meaning of those words. Nor was I interested in studying their meaning. What I experienced was their beauty and their different, life-giving ideal. I wanted to be one of the blessed ones, especially the pure of heart, because they see God.

Experienced-Centered Reading

In this chapter and the next we will try to show what it is to read the New Testament both as an expression of the Christ experience and as a means of entering into this experience. To assist us in this experience-centered reading we will employ as best we can Taoist and Mahayana Buddhist consciousness. We do this not only because these are the two great far eastern mindsets which we have been following throughout this book, but also because they are both totally centered on enlightenment. Lao Tzu, Chuang Tzu, Shakyamuni Buddha, the many Zen masters like Lin Chi (Japanese: Rinzai) and Dogen are truly of the highest level of consciousness advancement. From our own experience we know that they can greatly assist us in better knowing our Christian hero, Jesus of Nazareth.

Before commenting directly on the beatitudes passages in Luke and Matthew we would like to again insist that the main source of all Jesus' teaching was his enlightenment. He taught from his own experience. This is why he was said to have taught "as one who had authority and not as the scribes" (Mk 1:22) who taught by quoting others. One of the great religious experiences of the world was that of Jesus after he was baptized by John in the River Jordan. It was then that "the heavens opened" for him, which is to say that the higher wisdom which had been hidden up to that time was now made clear. In a word, he was enlightened. The essential part of this towering experience was that he realized his identity with the infinite principle of his life and of all life. This wonderfully advanced self-identification is expressed in terms appropriate to the culture in which he lived: "You are my beloved Son; with you I am pleased" (Mk 1:11). This is form consciousness (the Son) finding itself as form–formless. Later on it will be even more clearly expressed as "I and the Father are one." To express the same Father-Son consciousness, Lao Tzu (chapter 52) uses the term "mother" for the formless principle and "child" for the form.

That the Jordan River experience was one of oneness is seen in the appearance of the dove. "He saw the heavens opened and the Spirit descending upon him like a dove" (Mk 1:10). In the Hebrew scriptures a dove is not a symbol of peace but of love, which is the oneness of form and formless (Son and Father) in the one movement (spirit) of life.

Then Mark continues, ". . . the Spirit immediately drove him out into the wilderness." This means not just that Jesus was physically led to go out into the desert, but also that his awareness was so expanded that he moved into an inner wilderness. There he spent forty days to integrate his new horizon into his body, emotions, imagination, mind and all other movements of his being. During this time he was so filled with the life force that he really did not need any material food, so he fasted. Also, he was in communion with all the lower and higher forms of life. "He was with wild beasts and angels waited upon him" (Mk 1:13).

Finally, he was "tempted by Satan," Mark says. What is this Satan and how was he tempted? The fact was that, while going through the process of consciousness expansion and integration, Jesus simultaneously experienced the interaction and counteraction of his old habits, i.e. his

ordinary conventional patterns of thinking, feeling, etc. He
was tested and pulled by the power of the remaining old
habits which, in his new state of being, are delusion and
pride. This power that resists the movement of the spirit
was designated by Mark as "Satan."

The very fact that he could still be actually tempted
seems to clearly mean that this experience was not yet totally perfect. Absolute perfection, it would seem, came only
with his death and resurrection. However, these temptations themselves contributed to advancing Jesus' consciousness to such a high level that the teaching he gave from it
during his public life could easily be used later by his first
disciples in order to communicate the definitive enlightenment he came to in resurrection. One of the most startling
characteristics of this teaching was its insistent demand for
a change in consciousness and value system.

Transvaluation of Values

This "transvaluation of values" is an expression of the
tragic prophet of the existentialists, Friedrich Nietzsche.
This genius clearly saw that what Jesus of Nazareth did was
to establish a whole new value system. That this is Jesus'
clear intent is found in the famous synopsis of his whole
teaching given by Mark immediately after his account of
the enlightenment by the river. "The time is fulfilled and
the kingdom of God is at hand; repent and believe the
gospel" (1:15). The gospel, the good news, is that not only
Jesus himself but all of us are beloved children of the Father. We are all God incarnate. (Remember that we are
giving the far eastern interpretation.) We are all form–
formless. Jesus invites us all to entrust ourselves to this
gospel and to come to share in his own self-identification.

However, for us to actually enter into this awareness

we must "repent." As is well known these days this "repent," *metanoite,* means a radical shift of consciousness *Ou*
about ourselves and life. It entails a change not only of our
self-identification but of our whole value system and philosophy of life. The state of advanced consciousness Jesus
is in forces him to demand this *metanoia.* As we shall see,
he challenges us to transcend the very distinction between
good and evil so cherished by those (i.e. us) who have risen
up from the subconscious state of Eden. The beatitudes
represent a radical call to *metanoia.*

The mind-shaking inversion of values of the Christ
consciousness is more striking in Luke's version of the
beatitudes. So we will take this first.

Blessed are you poor, for yours is the kingdom
   of God. *the other kingdom*
Blessed are you that hunger now, for you shall
   be satisfied. *in new age everything will be better*
Blessed are you that weep now, for you shall
   laugh. *rejoice*
Blessed are you when men hate you, and when
   they exclude you and revile you, and cast
   out your name as evil, on account of the
   Son of Man!
Rejoice in that day, and leap for joy, for behold
   your reward is great in heaven; for so their
   fathers did to the prophets.
But woe to you that are rich, for you have
   received your consolation.
Woe to you that are full now, for you shall
   hunger.
Woe to you that laugh now, for you shall
   mourn and weep.

Woe to you, when all men speak well of you,
for so their fathers did to the false prophets.

—*Luke 6:20–26*

Actual poverty, hunger, weeping in sadness, being hated and reviled are hardly considered to be situations that make us happy by any society and certainly not by Hebrew society. Yet Jesus presents them as things that are intimately connected with happiness and even joy. The Greek word for these blessed persons, *makarioi,* can give us some hint of what this intimate connection is. Originally, *makarioi* indicated the blessed state of the gods in contrast to humans. Therefore, these "evils" are said to somehow bring us to divine happiness. Briefly put, poverty, hunger, weeping and persecution can all so shatter our complacency that we are forced to abandon the *incomplete* self-consciousness of the fourth evolutionary stage and rise up to the awareness of our own "divinity." They open us out so that we can realize that we are "sharers" in the divine nature (2 Pet 1:4). These "evils" are the instruments that can force us to die to the exclusive self and rise to the fullness of life. Therefore, they are truly *valuable.* On the other hand, the "good" things, viz. riches, abundant food, laughter and esteem, because they easily lull us into remaining in our incomplete consciousness, are not valuable, but even harmful. Woe to those who enjoy them!

These "blesseds" and "woes" of Luke are powerful and do shake up our value system. But the beatitudes as given in Matthew, especially the places where they differ from Luke, present an even more subtle, elevated teaching and seem to lead us even deeper into the actual Christ consciousness of Jesus of Nazareth. Just as we began this section by quoting from Nietzsche, so we can end it by giving the title of one of his greatest works. It beautifully synopsizes the teaching of Jesus in Matthew's sermon on the mount: *Beyond Good and Evil, Prelude to a Philosophy of the Future.*

Beyond Values

We can note here that both in Luke and in Matthew the sermon on the mount is presented not as given before a large crowd of indiscriminate followers, but as a teaching to the inner group of disciples to whom Jesus entrusts his deepest, truly enlightened communication. "Seeing the crowds, he went up on the mountain, and when he sat down, his disciples came to him. And he opened his mouth and taught them" (Mt 5:1–2). Scripture scholars point out that Jesus saw the huge, passing crowds that came to be healed (Mt 4:22–25) and went away up on the mountain. His disciples followed and he was able to open his heart to them. He gave them *esoteric* teaching, in the best sense of the term. Esoteric simply means inner. "Exoteric" teaching deals more with the outer aspects of life. In this chapter we are trying to read the scripture text with esoteric eyes, because in the gospels it is the inner reality of life, especially its hidden infinite reality, that Jesus is trying to teach us.

Actually, Jesus had to keep the clear expression of this inner teaching from the crowds, because it would shock them too much. The gospel of Mark in particular tells us repeatedly how Jesus tried to guard his esoteric communication and how he taught the crowds only in parables. To his disciples he says, "To you has been given the secret of the kingdom of God, but for those outside everything is in parables" (Mk 4:11). The reason for this is that a clear exposure of his advanced consciousness sounds utterly unintelligible or false or even blasphemous to the ordinary egoic consciousness, especially of his time. Moreover, what he was actually teaching meant death to the very ego awareness they identified with. The fourth level (ego) consciousness, especially personified in the scribes and also within the Pharisees, did reject and finally kill him. Christians themselves must constantly "be on guard against idols" (1 Jn 5:21), the false principles and values of the incomplete self-identification consciousness.

"Blessed are the poor in spirit for theirs is the kingdom of heaven" (Mt 5:3). The nuance of difference between Luke's "poor" and Matthew's "poor in spirit" would seem to be significant. "In spirit" clearly accents the inner state of a person. One modern Japanese version phrases it very well: "Blessed are those who know their own poverty." The poverty in spirit that Jesus so wants to share with us is the experience of ourselves as *no thing,* as formless, as the infinite principle of life. To the Mahayana mind of Master Dogen, poverty of spirit would clearly be "the dropping off of mind and body" which he so insisted upon. This existential poverty results in rising to true life in the one great, all-powerful flow of life. This joyful experience of be-ing in the flow is precisely the blessedness of the reign of God, which Jesus promises to the poor in spirit.

Lao Tzu, too, hearing these words of Jesus, would smile and perhaps repeat the beginning words of his Chapter 16.

I enter into utmost emptiness (poverty of spirit)
and maintain the stillness wholeheartedly.
All things are moving together
and I contemplate their cyclic movement.
(God's reign)

He also agrees with the "woes" of Luke when he continues:

> When one does not know the eternal
> (because of the complacency of riches, esteem, *14*
>   etc.)
> blindness causes disaster. cf J ohn

Lin Chi, too, experienced what it is to be "poor in spirit."
He calls it being "a person of no title." He urges us to join
him in a self-identification beyond all categories.
14

> Over your mass of reddish flesh
> there sits a true being who has
> no title. He is all the time coming
> in and out through your sense
> organs. If you have not yet
> testified to this reality, Look! Look!

> (authors' translation)

The inner teaching of Jesus consistently calls us to find
ourselves as beyond all categories. "The Son of Man has
nowhere to lay his head." The title Jesus so often uses for
himself, Son of Man, refers to the mysterious figure in the
prophecy of Daniel (7:13ff). It not only indicates that he is
the person of eternal power as written in the prophets, but
also certainly shows that Jesus is pointing to himself as a
model for all humans. He is our model especially because
he "has nowhere to lay his head." He is the void, the
formless, truly poor in spirit. In this consciousness even
the seemingly absolutely valid categories of right and
wrong, beautiful and ugly, even good and evil disappear.
There is nothing but one flow of be-ing, formless to form to

formless to . . . All relative judgments are lost. A person goes beyond values. As Chuang Tzu says, "So the sage harmonizes with both right and wrong and rests in heaven, the equalizer" (Chapter 2). The enlightenment experience called "poor in spirit" produces what we can call an absolute, a transvaluational consciousness. As Lao Tzu says, "The sage has no fixed state of mind" (Chapter 49). The Mahayana *Diamond Sutra* puts it very well, "The awakened mind is not fixed anywhere nor does it exclusively abide." Finally, in Zen, this state is called *mushin* (Chinese: *wu-hsin*) which means a mind that is non-fixed and moves freely and equally over all manifestations of the one flow. This does not mean that in the relative order these categories do not remain. They do. A strong dose of poison is judged "evil" for the human body. A nutritious meal is "good" for the human body. But there is no *absolute* good or evil, beautiful or ugly, right or wrong. For an enlightened person these relative judgments and all value systems are made within the context of the life-giving flow of the *yin–yang* movement. A person who experiences poverty in spirit is the free and dynamic person we described in Chapter 9. Such a person knows that no snowflake ever falls in the wrong place. Or, to use the *haiku* poem of the poet Issa, whose *poverty* had him sleeping in a room where the snow blew in to cover his bedclothes:

> How welcome!
> Even the snow on my bedclothes—
> The Pure Land.

The Pure Land is a beautiful Mahayana expression for the reign of God. It is this beatific vision, the pearl beyond price (values) that Jesus calls us to in poverty of spirit.

Once we realize that *the beatitudes passage is a call to*

enlightenment, the interpretation of each verse becomes rather obvious. The same radical teaching is repeated with each beatitude having its own nuance. "Those who mourn" are people who, like Shakyamuni Buddha, start from existential human suffering and end in the true comfort of enlightenment. "The meek" are those whose ego attachment is totally dissolved by the experience of the infinite. These are not unmoving (and dead) but flexible (and alive). They refuse to be drawn into violent confrontation. Rather, they draw all hostile energy flow into the one flow by their suppleness. "Those who hunger and thirst for holiness" have activated the naked stirring of the heart within themselves. They will certainly be filled with the fullness of life. "The merciful" are unconditional in their loving will to bring all to share in their experience of oneness. "The pure of heart" are like spring flowers that place no obstacle to the infinite flow of life they are manifesting. There is no preoccupation, above all no self-centered consciousness. Thus they see themselves as the very formless they give form to. *Shalom* is usually translated as peace. But this Hebrew peace is not just the "tranquility of order," as Augustine's definition has it, but rather a condition in which nothing is lacking, a state of completion. "Peacemakers," then, are those who have come to infinite completion and lead others to the same. "Those who are persecuted" are the ones who learn, like Jesus himself, the folly of the cross. Rejected by those of exclusive ego-consciousness, they stand like a beacon to guide the world to its evolutionary climax. To use the phrase Jesus employs just two verses below, "You are the light of the world" (Mt 5:14).

13. Wine Tasting

And wine to gladden
the human heart.

—Psalm 104:15

Modern scholars speak of the first half of the gospel of John, from the end of the prologue to the end of chapter 12, as the book of signs, and count seven major sign-actions of Jesus written in this book. Others count differently and make the whole of the passion, death and resurrection event as the seventh greatest sign. For our purpose either numeration is fine because it is the very idea of sign that we want to stress. At the end of the gospel John writes, "Now Jesus did many other signs in the presence of the disciples, which are not written in this book; but these are written that you may believe that Jesus is the Christ, the Son of God, and that, believing, you may have life in his name." Sign here is not just an external indication like a neon light telling us that this building is a restaurant. Rather, it is an event on the outer level of life that graphically displays what can happen on the inner level. When Jesus heals someone's physical blindness, this is a sign that he is here to take away the blindness of our incomplete consciousness and lead us to the light of infinite experience. His giving bread and fish is a sign of his giving us the only experience that can satisfy the human heart. John is very clear about the "sign" character of all of Jesus' actions. He is actually giving to us the key, not only as to how to read his gospel, but the synoptics as well. Everything related about Jesus in the four gospels is sign. Until we get to the inner, esoteric meaning of all the passages, we are not reading the gospels

177

as they were intended. To truly read these four gospels
means that we understand the inner teachings of Jesus and
entrust our very selves to him. Believing this, we will have
life in his name. Reading the gospels as books of signs is the
same as reading them for their inner, esoteric meaning.

The First Sign

As another example of this kind of reading we can
briefly take up the "first two of his signs," which are given
at the beginning of John, chapter 2. (We will use the NAB
translation.)

> On the third day there was a wedding at Cana in
> Galilee, and the mother of Jesus was there. Jesus
> and his disciples had likewise been invited to the
> celebration.

When these lines are read as describing a sign, every word
takes on deeper meaning, a meaning John certainly intended. "The third day" has to do with rising to fullness of
life, which for Jesus, our archetype, happened on the third
day. "Wedding" refers to entering into the oneness of life
in the spirit. It refers to the wedding of form consciousness
and formless consciousness in one human self-identification. This is not a wedding of two things, but of yin and
yang principles of life in the one life flow, the spirit. "And
the mother of Jesus was there" points out something of
immense importance. There is a tradition that Mary was
the aunt, Jesus the cousin of the groom. This would account for their being there and for Mary's concern about
how things went. But all this is sign. Mary is the embodied
archetype of openness to the spirit. This is the positive
meaning of her immaculate conception. Without this

openness there can be no wedding in the spirit. She must be there one way or another.

> At a certain point the wine ran out, and Jesus'
> mother told him, "They have no more wine."
> Jesus replied, "Woman, how does this concern of
> yours involve me? My hour has not yet come."
> His mother instructed those waiting on table, "Do
> whatever he tells you."

In all cultures wine is connected with joy and celebration. The psalmist speaks of "wine to gladden the human heart" (Ps 104:15). As a sign, then, wine is the joy of union in the Spirit, the joy of life in its fullness. It is fitting, then, for Mary, who is pure openness to the Spirit, to ask for this wine. "My hour" is clearly a technical term in John for Jesus' time of going to the Father through his passion and death. The hour refers to the event by which Jesus' own true "wedding" takes place in resurrection, when he entered into perfect light and unlimited power. This is when he became the leader to salvation for all who entrust themselves to him. So, by his remarks to his mother, Jesus actually explains the inner meaning of the sign that he is about to perform. His words are not a refusal to provide wine, but an explanation that what he is about to do is a sign of the true joy that he will bring to all through his own experiential leadership and inner influence.

When she tells the waiters to do whatever he tells them, Mary is again true to her character of openness. She knows that Jesus is filled with the Spirit and therefore tells all to simply follow him. This is all that human beings need to do to come to the joy of the wedding.

After this Jesus changed the water in six stone jars into wine, thus providing something like one hundred and

twenty gallons of wine for the celebration. When the head-
waiter tasted this new wine, he said to the groom, "People
usually serve the choice wine first. . . . What you have done
is keep the choice wine until now." So Jesus provides not
just a superabundance of wine (joy) but wine of the highest
quality—the supreme and unlimited joy of experiencing
oneself as infinite power and light in human manifestation.
In this actual written text Jesus and John are teamed together to communicate this wonderful wine. The same is to
be said of all the four gospels and of Paul and Jesus in the
Pauline letters. What we are trying to do in this chapter on
experience-centered reading is to help all to a higher and
richer level of *wine tasting,* until we become intoxicated
with the joy of the true wedding celebration.

A Day of Light and Power

"For the word of God is living and active, sharper
than any two-edged sword . . ." (Heb 4:12). The word that
is primarily meant here (and in similar passages: Eph 6:17;
Rev 1:16; 2:12; Is 49:2) is the word as it proceeds from the
mouth of the prophet, especially of Jesus. This word is
living and active. It is creative and a release of power. We
see this idea of power in the first word of God in the Bible,
"Then God said, 'Let there be light,' and there was light"
(Gen 1:3). The *word* of Jesus refers not just to verbal words,
but to all that he said and did. These are communicated to
us primarily in the written scripture texts. Thus our gospels
certainly share in the light and power of Jesus himself. As
to the vital question of how we are to release this creative
power from the written word, investigate mindfulness as
developed in the next chapter. For now we will take two
more passages and read them in an esoteric way using the
light from Taoist/Mahayana consciousness and from the

evolutionary analysis of spiritual development. The first is about the disciples' great day of light and power.

Although for Christians the passage of Jesus to the Father through death and resurrection is in a very real sense the greatest of all human events, nevertheless, in another sense, the Pentecost event is of at least equal importance, because it is the great definitive enlightenment of Jesus' disciples. This is the day on which the disciples came to actually share in the light and power of the resurrection. The day that Jesus, together with his disciples, had been longing for. A day that is important for us today because when we commemorate the event, we are actualizing it. It is now our turn.

Even though preparation for Pentecost started the very first time the disciples met Jesus, the final and essential opening out to the Spirit began with the drastic shock therapy of Jesus' death and the shattering light of his resurrection. It culminated in the intense nine days which followed his ascension into heaven. "He charged them not to depart from Jerusalem, but to wait for the promise of the Father. . . . 'Before many days you shall be baptized with the Holy Spirit' " (Acts 1:4–5). So the disciples returned to the upper room to make the first and greatest novena of prayer. The room itself was charged with divine energy because it was there they had celebrated the last paschal meal, the first "Lord's supper," and heard the final outpouring of the heart of Christ. There they all "with one accord devoted themselves to prayer," waiting for the Lord. At the very center of this waiting for the Spirit was Mary, who was not only the mother of Jesus, but also his first and greatest disciple. As already noted, Mary is the archetype of openness to the Spirit, just as Jesus is the archetype of those filled with the Spirit (the anointed; in Greek, *hoi Christoi*). It was Mary's spirit which governed

the nine days of preparation until finally, on the fiftieth
day (in Greek, *he pentecoste hemera*) after the resurrection,
the immense event took place.   *Pente.*

This feast was originally a harvest feast celebrating the
first fruits of the grain harvest roughly seven weeks after
the Passover. The symbolism, of course, fits perfectly, for
it became the day when the first fruits of Jesus' passage to
the Father were actualized definitively. The very number
fifty indicates the same, because five is the fruitful number.
(Fruit trees have five petals. Those of beauty without fruit
have three or six.) Ten is the round number, the number of
fullness. This event is truly a fiftieth day, a day of fruit-
full-ness. In later Judaism the feast was also the anniver-
sary of the giving of the law of the Spirit. This law is not
something imposed from the outside, but rather simply the
very law of our being arising to our consciousness. We are
made to be God-in-manifestation. When this reality arises
to awareness we are enlightened, seeing our true nature.

Aside from the long speech by Peter, the account of the
event in Acts is very brief. Yet, even in these few verses, the
immense dynamism of what took place is apparent. That
morning there was such a tremendous energy flow that it
sounded "like the rush of a mighty wind, and it filled all the
house where they were sitting" (v. 2). The whole place
became an energy field of such force that something like
the fire that we see in electrical storms gathered together
and "there appeared to them tongues as of fire, distributed
and resting on each one of them" (v. 3). In a very plausible
account of this event, given by one modern American psychic, the disciples are depicted as being so charged up physically that their hair literally stood on end and electrical
sparks flashed between them when they happened to touch
one another. Even restricting ourselves to just the scriptural account, it is clear that there was a visible manifesta-

tion of an immense release of energy at all levels of the human being of each disciple. "They were all filled with the Holy Spirit" (v. 4). The Spirit (*ruah* in Hebrew, *spiritus* in Latin) is the breath of life, the actual movement of the absolute into manifestation. In the deepest sense of the word this was a breath-taking experience.

The years of public life with Jesus, the shock of his death which shattered their narrow worldview, the all-powerful presence of the risen Christ, and the final intense preparation with Mary have removed all obstacles within the disciples. They are in the state of great openness. This allows the wellspring of life present within them (as in all humans) to gush forth in a mighty flow. In the light of their very own being they discover their oneness with Jesus and with all beings. They see their own truth and the truth of all in the enlightenment of the "Spirit of Truth."

Only then do they at last speak with the authority of Christ, i.e. from the foundation of the ultimate spiritual experience. ". . . and they began to speak in other tongues as the Spirit gave them utterance" (v. 6). And all the people who came together when they heard the great sound were amazed to "hear them telling in our own tongues the mighty works of God" (v. 11). There are two possible interpretations of the remarkable communication that happened that day. It could have been much like what happens at present day charismatic meetings when some people are so moved by the profound energy flow to which they have entrusted themselves that they break forth in a speech not their own. Sometimes this stream of speech has been identified as one of the many human languages. This would mean that the disciples were speaking in languages unintelligible to themselves. Such an interpretation would seem to keep the event at only the psychic level.

The explanation that we favor is that the disciples

simply spoke in their own language, Aramaic. But what
they said came from the experience of the very wellspring
of all human life and activity. The Aramaic words were so
full of power that they went directly to the deepest heart of
the hearers and activated their inner powers so much that
within themselves the hearers converted the message into
their own language. It was heart to heart communication so
powerful that it was even understood intellectually by all.

However one interprets this communication, the
whole event was clearly a sublime enlightenment experience. In Japanese Zen there is the expression *dai go tettei.*
Dai means great; *go,* enlightenment; *tettei* literally means
piercing to the bottom. This is the great experience that
goes definitively to the very source of all being. For the
disciples it was certainly such an enlightenment, the experience of eternal life. And since it released all the flow of
divine life, it was also the great empowerment. From this
time on the disciples became apostles, communicating the
light and power of Christ to an ever widening circle of
fellow humans. It was out of this apostolic preaching that
the four gospels arose. These four texts, then, are primarily
not a history of the life of Jesus of Nazareth, but a presentation of the Christ consciousness through the skillfully ar-
ranged account of details from Jesus' life. The gospels are
enlightenment and empowerment documents.

As a final example of reading the gospels with esoteric
eyes we can take a section from the conclusion of Mark's
gospel:

> And Jesus said to his disciples: "Go into all the
> world and preach the gospel to the whole creation.
> He who believes and is baptized will be saved; but
> he who does not believe will be condemned. And

these signs will accompany those who believe: in
my name they will cast out demons; they will
speak in new tongues; they will pick up serpents,
and if they drink any deadly thing, it will not hurt
them; they will lay their hands on the sick, and
they will recover" (16:15–18).

Jesus is presented here as telling the disciples about
what their ministry will be after the Pentecost event. "To
the whole creation" is a significant phrase in relation to the
Christ enlightenment experience. Not only humans, but all
"creatures," all the ten thousand forms, are seen to be one
flow of life. People who are in the first glow of enlightenment always say that rocks, trees and all things are new and
different. Everything shares in the ineffable flow. The disciples of Jesus are to proclaim this good news to all. "Baptism" is plunging one's whole being into that powerful
movement of the Spirit that ends in the new life of fully
actualized consciousness/be-ing. Anyone who refuses to
submit to this life-force condemns herself/himself to wal-
low in the pain and fruitless struggle of the false self.

"And these signs will accompany those who believe."
Now, not just the actions of Jesus but also the actions of
those who have fully entrusted themselves to the Spirit of
Jesus are called signs. This very word "sign" is highly significant. The actions that are enumerated in this passage
point to a higher level of light and power than is needed to
perform the actions themselves. Each one of the actions is
hardly more than an activation of the psychic level of the
evolutionary stage, with probably some actuation of the
sixth (devic) level as well. But to limit the attainment of the
disciples of Jesus to mere psychic healing would be to
drastically reduce the very attainment of Jesus himself and

the immense movement of the Spirit he inaugurated. No, these are signs of the highest levels of life actuation. We will accept and rejoice in them as such.

One more preliminary note is that the actions mentioned are unusual and thus possess special sign value, but as the church has always taught, the whole lives of Christians are witness to the gospel, or at least should be. All our actions are to be expressions of Christ consciousness and power.

"In my name they will cast out demons." This sign is given first, and in one way of looking at it, it is the most profound. The ultimate demon to be cast out is attachment to the very consciousness that differentiates between angels and demons. As we discussed in the section on the beatitudes, the rising to ultimate awareness takes us beyond good and evil. Demons themselves, whatever they are, are also the flow of life and ultimately obey the inner and higher harmony. The highest casting out of demons is to sublimate them all to the one great flow, to experience them too as God-in-manifestation.

"They will speak in new tongues." We just discussed this in the Pentecost section. Here we can note that language, as we have it, is actually a grid through which we process the stream of life data as it comes to us. Our great variety of human languages have all been created by the differentiating, categorizing intellect. As such they can never grasp or express the ultimate reality of life. The "new tongues" indicated here could be languages that are different from the first disciples' native Aramaic or Greek. However, ultimately what is new about the language they used to preach the gospel is that it actually communicates the inexpressible light and power of the absolute. Whatever "new tongues" were used are only signs of this mysterious new communication.

"They will pick up serpents." The sign of picking up serpents indicates that superb state in which a fully actualized person is able to freely employ any level of our old friend, the serpent power, i.e. consciousness. The cover of a recent book by the Catholic priest Swami Amaldas has on it a truly Indian picture of Jesus with a seven headed serpent forming a halo over his head. This indicates that in Jesus the consciousness of each of the seven energy centers (*chakras*) is fully sublimated. These centers now provide the free and easy energy flow through which he works in us and in all creation. Those, too, who entrust themselves to Jesus, ultimately experience the actualization of this free power.

"And if they drink any deadly thing, it will not hurt them." This simply represents a further generalization of the principle that, for those fully established in Christ consciousness, nothing in the world can harm them. There is no longer anything to fear. This is what Paul experienced and then expressed in his personalist language, saying, "We know that God makes all things work together for the good of those who love him" (Rom 8:28). Or, as Andrew Weil puts it, "Mystical experience is the mirror image of negative paranoia. It sees 'the universe is a conspiracy organized for my benefit.' "[1]

"They will lay their hands on the sick, and they will recover." This is a truly beautiful sign, and what it signifies is clear and infinitely comforting. We recall the touching scene one Saturday evening when the whole town with their sick were gathered outside Peter's house. Jesus came and "laid his hands on every one of them and healed them"

(Lk 4:40). The energy filled hands that Jesus of Nazareth laid on the world are now the hands of his disciples. Their enlightening power heals the sickness of all four levels of human development: the bodily, the image–emotional, the social–communicative, and the mental–egoic. This is accomplished by drawing humans up to the infinite source of all and into the one harmonious flow of eternal life.

14. Mind You

> "I couldn't see anything
> but the hydrangea."
>
> —*Japanese student*

A: My connection with the practice of mindfulness is both mysterious and ordinary. In the summer of 1977 on my way back to Taiwan from Brazil, I stopped over in West Paterson, New Jersey to visit our sisters there. Just two days before my departure I asked an American sister to drive me to a bookstore so I could pick up some books for our community in Taiwan. When we got to the store the sister told me that I could only spend forty minutes there because she had another engagement. This made me rather disappointed and worried. Since I had been away from the English speaking world for almost ten years and had no idea whatsoever about any names of books or authors, how could I do book shopping in forty minutes?

I picked out one book after another as best I could and ended up buying quite a pile. Before sending them by sea to Taiwan, I chose one of the smallest ones to be my companion on the trip back to Taiwan. It had the simple, easy English title: *The Miracle of Mindfulness* by Thich Nhat Hanh. This little book unexpectedly played an extraordinary role during my journey. All the while on the trip home it brought me so much peace and joy that I found the journey was very short. Since then I have recommended the book to I don't know how many people. Whenever people ask me about spiritual reading books, *The Miracle of Mindfulness* is always first on the list. Here we would

like to share some considerations about this miraculous
power of mindfulness on our life journey.

We are very aware that our book has been organized in
a very western way. The ideas and explanations have been
put first and the practice last. As is so often the case, the
east is the other way around. In the classical Zen pattern,
an aspirant is taught how to sit, to chant, to work. Then,
only after some real level of insight-experience is reached,
is the inner theory of Buddhism explored. But in the west
people do seem to need a "learner's permit," to use
Wilber's felicitous phrase. We need to explain things to the
reasoning mind which so dominates the western scene. The
mind has to be assured that the pursuit in question is not
regressive or pathological and, above all, not unreasonable,
and then it gives us permission to practice. Since this book
was first envisioned as mainly for westerners, perhaps its
actual order is acceptable. Deep in our hearts, though, we
know that all that has been said so far is quite useless
without serious practice. This chapter, then, is by far the
most important. If we are to actually rise from self-consciousness to super-consciousness, practice is the *only*
path. To be just reasonable is, sadly enough, completely
unreasonable.

Attention–Actualization

Up to now we have often used expressions such as
life-force, the one dynamic force, the one dynamic flow,
the power of the word, and empowerment, etc. When we
come right down to it, what we are primarily talking about
is the power *within ourselves.* Each one of us has the power
within to move up the levels of being/consciousness to the
fullness of life, the spirit life. In fact this power within *is* the

spirit. The crucial question, then, is how to release this
power. Just thinking about it may bring it to the surface
somewhat, but thinking can never release it. The one practice above all that can activate the great evolutionary force
within us is *attention*. What you put your attention to happens. And it happens according to the manner of attention.
Pure, single-minded attention infallibly brings actualization. This is the law Jesus of Nazareth enunciates so clearly
when he says, "Truly, I say to you, whoever says to the
mountain, 'Be taken up and cast into the sea,' and does not
doubt his heart but believes that what he says will come to
pass, it will be done for him" (Mk 12:23). In one of Carlos
Castaneda's books, Don Juan tells Carlos that if we hold a
thought in our minds to the exclusion of everything else,
that thought becomes a command.

The Tibetans, Indians, and all those who have dealt
directly with the energy centers (*chakras*) always teach that
the way to release the energy from any one center is to put
one's awareness on that center. Pure Land Buddhism has
the *nembutsu* (in Chinese, *nien fo*) as its great path to the
land of light and bliss. *Nem* is the verb to mind. *Butsu* is
Buddha, the enlightened one. Total and constant attention
to the Buddha, brought about mainly through mantric
chanting, is an infallible way to entrance into the Pure
Land (state) of enlightenment, power and joy. To repeat,
what we put our minds to happens. And if our minding,
our attention is distracted, mixed up, fuzzy and pulled in
contradictory directions, nothing will happen. There is
deep truth in the following example. Say that ten people go
on a picnic and that one of them is deathly afraid of snakes.
This very fear keeps the person attentive to and looking for
snakes everywhere. The result is that the one who runs into
a snake is this person, this fearful attentiveness.

Mindfulness

The practice above all others is mindfulness. This "mind" is not just the mental mind but the process we use when we "mind the baby." We mind a baby with all the powers of our being: body, voice, hearing, all the senses, emotions, reason, intuition, our whole complex human composite. The basic practice which we are describing calls for the full mind, total attention. Granted, then, that mind-fulness will bring actualization, what are we to put our mind to?

The only "object" worthy of our full and total attention is life itself. We all want to really live, to be fully and gloriously alive. In fact, that is what life is all about. Since actualization of a power is brought about through attention, the only thing that merits our absolute and unalloyed attention is the life-force itself, the spirit, the *yin-yang* movement of *ch'i.* This will bring us to life. Furthermore, what is of supreme practical importance is that concretely speaking this means *attention to our own here and now living,* our individual *tao.* It means being fully aware of actions like breathing, sitting, eating, walking, talking, etc. In everything, being aware is being alive. To be fully aware is to be fully alive. The ever urgent journey up the ladder of consciousness can be begun anywhere. Let us begin with breathing.

Breathing

No other human action is so favored by spiritual masters of the east as breathing. All eastern systems of spiritual practice use it as an essential element. We have already mentioned how a Zen beginner's first inner practice is to count the breath with full attention not so much on the counting but on each act of breathing. Again, this must be

one's full attention without concern for anything else.
Since this is the first example we are taking we will go into
the whole process in detail.

As always we start with relaxation. As you begin meditation, you relax your body with only enough nerve and
muscle tension to maintain the meditation posture you
have chosen. This relaxation is of the greatest practical
importance because, in effect, it is a physical letting go of
everything else but quiet sitting. It is a bodily commitment
to this here and now sitting. Physical relaxation has an
immediate effect on one's whole human composite. It is
especially effective in reducing psychological resistance to
that energy flow which advances our consciousness. But
there is one physical movement you cannot stop, breathing, so let this be your point of attention. The path of
mindfulness is always the path of simplification. This
means not only that the activity one chooses to focus on is
this here and now single type of action (breathing), but also
this *one* act of breathing, forgetting the ones past and the
ones to come.

Another feature of this simple attention is that it puts
aside all thought of purpose and goal. Even the devotional
thought of doing this for Jesus has no place once you move
into the practice itself. Of course you are being mindful of
your breathing in order to advance along the evolutionary
course to Christ consciousness. There is no need to deny
this at all. But also there is no need to think about it or to
consciously intend it as you sit. On the contrary, such
thoughts are just as corrosive of the bare attention you are
practicing as the thought of the date you have set up for
later in the day. The thought of other, lesser, but not wrong
motives must also go—motives like success, desire for a
spiritual experience, the esteem of your teacher. Single-
mindedness is so free from the thought of any motive that

if, while you are deep in meditation, a person were to ask you "What are you doing?" you would easily answer, "I'm watching my breath." But if the person continued, "What are you doing that for?" you would stare blankly and just reply, "I'm watching my breath to watch my breath."

Feelings of like and dislike must be quietly suppressed. All judgments too, and comparisons are out: "This is great," "This is stupid," "This is better than yesterday," "I'm not getting anywhere," etc., etc. Your mind is not to be preoccupied or concerned with any such ideas. Actually, the only thing that is happening is the breath flowing in, flowing out right now. This is your life.

This radical simplification of attention is essential in order to progress into and eventually through formless awareness to spirit consciousness. When we are completely focused on one thing or no thing, we are moving ourselves out of relational consciousness. All relational, categorical thinking demands two points (two terms) to establish the relationship. Bare attention to only one point or object will produce a state in which that point itself disappears, because there is nothing left for it to relate to. Formless consciousness is all that remains. This is the world (stage) of infinite oneness, power and joy. Spirit consciousness is when this awareness is again joined to our ordinary relational consciousness.

Breath Pilgrimage

Suppose now that you are moving into a state of bare attention, single-mindedness, what will happen? What are the signs that this is advancing you toward full life, toward perfect being/awareness? The first thing that you might feel, as very many do, is a letting down of your burden. The anxieties, fears, concerns, tensions and stress are gone.

They are no longer a part of your life right now. This is in itself a very great step and quite difficult for so many. It implies a real dying to the separate ego because your burden is all ego-created. A very great step indeed. Another experience that soon arises is a sense of being in contact with reality and of being at home. You might feel like saying to yourself, "This is it! This is life!" In fact for those who have difficulty just following their breath with their awareness we sometimes recommend saying "This is it" with each inhalation or exhalation or both. Care must be taken, though, not to think much about what you mean by the words.

As you become more proficient in bare attention, you will begin to be more and more conscious of the "stirring of the heart." Those words of the author of *The Cloud of Unknowing* are a very good description of the most important result of single-minded breathing. The "heart" here refers to the spirit within us, the power of infinite consciousness and the potential to be in a myriad of forms. It is the power by which we experience "God." Using typically western personalist language, Augustine expresses it well when he said, "Our hearts are made for Thee, O God, and they are restless until they rest in Thee." By our very being we are pilgrims of the absolute. This life force is released by our bare attention to any particular human manifestation of it—in this case, breathing. This is the evolutionary drive that empowers people to carry on years of severe spiritual practice. In recent times, some groups of mainly young western people are going off to make arduous Vajrayana (Tibetan) retreats three years long. What moves them is this power, the very will to live fully. It is the stirring of the heart that makes everything, in the broad sense of the word, prayer. Without it nothing is really prayer.

Also to be noted is that this stirring is a sign of a

believing heart. The whole practice of mindfulness in any form starts with faith that this action is life itself and can be a door of divine discovery. It is positive faith, not in the sense of the opposite of negative because this would be judgmental, but in the sense that it affirms the great truth of your being and challenges you to open wide to the discovery of life.

At this stage in the mindfulness path because you are touching the very life process itself, each breath becomes infinitely precious. You feel that there is no need for anything else but this breath. Nothing else is important. And each breath is made with profound reverence and care. A dignity, even a grandeur, enters into your act of breathing that is a sign of the ever ancient, ever rhythmic movement of life itself. At this stage one is beginning to taste what St. Paul means when he says that our bodies are the temple of the Holy Spirit. *he allowing the "breath" et H Sp. entrance.*

All that you have done from the initial body relaxation to the letting go of all judgments is oriented toward this stirring of the heart. Once it occurs in a fully conscious way you must be especially careful to not let in self-centered thoughts about how well you are doing, how you would like to share this with others, how much you enjoy this and want to maintain it and such. Just stay with the bare attention to this breath, to this breath, to . . . There is still great advancement to be made.

As a final note on the stirring we should mention that the full phrase from *The Cloud of Unknowing* is "the naked stirring of the heart." The author means that in the type of meditation he is teaching this stirring is not clothed in any words, images or even actions, like breathing. All these are put into a "cloud of forgetting." It is pure attention with no object at all. We can call it no thing attention. However, as a kind of fix for the poor mind the author does allow the clothing of some simple one syllable words. It is this pure, naked stirring of the heart that is certainly the main element in the Zen practice called in Japanese *shikan taza* (*shikan,* only or just; *ta,* hit; *za,* sit). This is just sitting without any real object. It is often taken up after some proficiency is reached in breathing attention. If a person after some time of following the breath feels drawn to this even more simplified practice, it is certainly excellent and most highly recommended.

New Levels

One of the first signs of a developing psychic consciousness is a change in one's sense of time. Very often clock time seems to shorten. What is actually happening is that the sense of time is lost because single-minded attention draws us out of our ordinary perception of relational events. As Angelus Silesius says, "Time is of your own making. Its clock ticks in your head. The moment you stop thought, time too stops dead." *but you do say, so the not all in your head*

As you continue to mind your breath with the power of the spirit you may very well notice how sensitive you are becoming in your daily life. Flowers, bird songs, trees and animals seem to affect you more and more. Your attunement with people increases, producing pain or happiness depending on the circumstances. All of these easily increase until psychic powers of pre-cognition, clairvoyance, insight and a great increase of work ability may all manifest stronger and stronger. This is a sign that your consciousness is moving up to the fifth or psychic level. These are the shamanistic powers or *siddhi.* Some people get so excited about and enamored with these powers that they fix their intention and attention at this level and never progress further. All this is fine as far as it goes, but it is

better to stay with your breathing mindfulness in all simplicity.

If you do, you will come to times when you start to
become breathing itself. Less and less is there my little
breath and more and more is there just breathing itself.
This is already the move into devic, archetypical consciousness. The sixth level. You become aware that your
breathing is actually the great creative, archetypical
breathing in manifestation. It is one with all breathing everywhere. You may not have such highly reflective or ana-
lytic thoughts about it. It's probably better not to. But the
experience is something cosmic and unifying with all
breathing. Your exclusive, differentiating self (breath)-
consciousness is now so eroded that you can identify your
self (breath) on the expansive devic level. Because this is
unitive it brings joy. However, it shouldn't stop here. As
you enter fully into just being breathing itself, a sense
begins to grow that each breath is life itself. That this
breath is not just breath but everything. It is, you are, life
itself! Your breathing is not just the manifestation of
breathing but has begun to be *experienced* as the manifestation of life itself. As always this is not a matter of intellectual understanding but of existential awareness. Here you
are at the highest level of devic consciousness. It may very
well be that this is the level John describes in his gospel
prologue as the Word "through whom all things are made."
It could also be called the "Son of Man" consciousness.
Total absorption in your breathing has led you to the highest archetypical level of life as it is being existentially manifested in each breath. This great devic or causal level is
still form and as such is limited. But at the same time each
breath is ultimately the embodiment of the *infinite* principle of life.

The expansion of consciousness and the loss of the

exclusive self which began with the simple counting of breath is now ready to enter awareness of the infinite principle itself. As the eighth Oxherd Picture has it, everything drops away, both breathing and self. Nothing is left but an empty circle. This is the "utmost emptiness" of Lao Tzu (Chapter 16), the "mind fasting" of Chuang Tzu (Chapter 4). After describing "mind fasting" as an experience of emptiness, Chuang Tzu exhorts us, "Look into that closed room, the empty chamber where brightness (full enlightenment) is born!" It is a room that is closed to all relational thinking, empty of all categories. As already mentioned, Zen masters describe the same final expansion of consciousness as the dropping off of mind and body. If you come to this state you will certainly understand the death of Jesus Christ.

So your breathing pilgrimage is over. The final step, your resurrection from formlessness to identification with life itself, is now to be accomplished by the spirit pure and simple. Of course, the whole pilgrimage from start to finish is the work of the spirit but here at its completion you are "led by the Spirit" in the fullest and purest sense of this phrase. Chuang Tzu describes this last transformation in his account of the final stages of enlightenment of a man by the name of Pu Liang Yi. The first line of the passage is about the loss of all form, the final death. The remaining lines are the resurrection.

> After nine days he was able to put aside life.
> After he had put aside life, he was able to see
>   with the clarity of dawn.
> With the clarity of dawn he was able to see
>   Oneness.
> Seeing Oneness he was able to transcend past
>   and present.

Transcending past and present he was able to
   enter
  into the state of neither-death-nor-life.
That which kills life does not die;
  that which gives life to life is not born.
Nothing it doesn't destroy; nothing it doesn't
   complete.

(Chapter 6, authors' translation)

We cannot dwell further on this final state of spiritual perfection. Enough has already been written, especially in Chapters 7 and 9. Here we would just remind you that it is both a dualistic and a non-dualistic state. As a non-dualistic, there is no you (subject) minding (verb) your breathing (object) as all separate. In actuality they are all one. As the Zen master Seng-T'san (*Sosan* in Japanese) says,

In the higher realm of true Suchness
There is neither "self" nor "other."
When direct identification is sought,
We can only say, "Not Two."[1]

You and all "others" are just one life flow. It is a state beyond words.

Also, before concluding, what we have described is a kind of textbook pattern of discovery. The actual pattern varies with each person. And the degree of experience varies. We can go in and out of the levels of the pattern without truly abiding in them. Finally, this description of the whole pilgrimage through the practical method of breath mindfulness is really too brief. However, we hope

enough has been outlined to show how mindfulness is truly
a way of fulfilling Jesus' great synopsis of the Christian
path, "Deny yourself, take up your cross and follow me."

General Characteristics

Before going on to further develop our assertion that
mindfulness is the basic practice, we pause to summarize
its general characteristics as they have appeared in the
account of breathing awareness. Mindfulness demands the
bringing together of all the powers of our human composite. The old ascetical term describes it perfectly as *re-col-
lection*. The first and extremely important preliminary step
is bodily *relaxation. Full attention* is then given to some
concrete life action such as breathing, walking, etc. This
means that mindfulness always implies a *simplification* of
the object of attention. This object is always *here and now*.
Even in the memory of some event of the Christ's life,
often with visualization, the act of memory and visualization is one's present action. The attention is *single-minded*.
It lays aside all thought of purpose or goal and all judgments and comparisons. It is without any preoccupation or
concern. In a word, it is *bare attention* and nothing more.

Pausing

The breathing practice we have just described refers
mainly to breathing during meditation time. There are
other very *simple,* natural activities that also recommend
themselves for the same type of mindfulness practice.
There is a beautiful story about an old lady in Japan who
was sick in bed and could not do her sitting practice. In-

stead, one night, while in pain, she gave her total attention to listening to a clock ticking. Early in the morning she came to true enlightenment.

Among these simple natural activities walking is very commonly used. In fact, longer periods of sitting meditation are often interspersed with slow, contemplative walking. Again, the practices of recollection, relaxation, here and now and bare attention must be followed. The great vipassana (insight) meditation path, which is being followed by many these days, focuses not only on breathing and walking but on any and all bodily, psychological and mental activities that arise during sitting. When Anthony de Mello described the bodily vipassana type meditation, he would smilingly say, "Lose your mind and come to your senses!" When distractions come, one becomes fully aware of them too, often by repeating "thinking, thinking . . ." or "hurting, hurting" or "hearing, hearing" until the mind is focused again and then can be returned to its chosen point of attention. We don't have space here to describe these practices in detail, only to refer you to the fine manuals of vipassana meditation that are quite available today. For walking mindfulness our *Miracle of Mindfulness* master, Nhat Hanh has put out *A Guide to Walking Meditation* which is far better put than anything we could write.

Although all these practices are done primarily within meditation time, their great immediate fruit is the enduring quality of consciousness which they produce. Awareness of life makes us alive, light, strong and able. Every effort should be made to maintain this consciousness in daily life. For this, *pausing* is most essential.

When Charlie Brown complained to Lucy during a baseball game that she didn't even catch a fly ball that fell right at her feet in left field, Lucy archly answered, "I was having my quiet time." Pausing for a moment of quiet

shouldn't, of course, cause inconvenience or work interruption, but to pause and recollect, relax, refocus your
attention is invaluable. If you are practicing breath mindfulness, pause to breathe with bare attention. The same
with walking or any other focal point. But pausing to enter
mindfulness is very well extended to anything that happens
in your day—to eating, drinking during a coffee break,
hearing a bird, looking at a child playing, feeling a cool
breeze. The result will be that gradually you will extend
this single-minded attention to whatever you are doing.
This is what the old Latin saying has exhorted us for centuries, "Age quod agis"—simply: "Do what you are
doing."

The practice and value of pausing is well expressed in
this grade school experience recounted by a Japanese college student.

It was one morning in June. After the rain the air
was grateful. As usual I was walking to school with
my bag. Men and children, even birds, grass,
leaves and flowers seemed happy. I don't know
why, but I felt happy. On my way to school, one
thing caught my eyes. It was a light purple colored
hydrangea. I *stopped* and looked at it. Till then I
had never noticed it. I looked at it, *stared* at it. I
felt any feelings or thoughts were disappearing
from my head and heart. *I couldn't see anything
but the hydrangea.* I felt my flesh and spirit was
drawing into it. And suddenly I returned to myself. That strange experience happened in a moment. I didn't understand the feeling and now I
can't describe it exactly. But it is certain that
something in my heart and something in the hydrangea became one. (Italics added.)

Who Is Breathing?

As we have already noted, mindfulness always implies a simplification of the object of attention. In our main example, we described the change of consciousness that can occur when a person gives full, non-judgmental attention to the act of breathing. The total object of attention was *what* is happening. Such single-minded attention truly can reveal the infinite power operating in everything. There is another element within the act of breathing that can advance consciousness to the spirit level. We can focus not so much on what but on *who* is breathing. Or, who is the one who is walking, eating, reading, etc.?

T: Here I would like to go into a bit more detail about the *kikunushi* practice already mentioned in Chapter 2. I had been doing zazen for over six months and had been working on the practice of following my breath with the syllable *mu.* I was doing this faithfully but really did not seem to be getting anywhere. There was another practice Yamada Roshi had spoken of and it had always caught my attention. It was a practice expressed in the Japanese question, "*Kikunushi, nani mono zo?*" "The one who is hearing, what kind of being is it?" (*Kiku* means to hear or to listen; *nushi* means lord, the one ultimately responsible.) One is to listen to any available sound and then ask this question. I was just about to leave for a Catholic Zen center in the mountains west of Tokyo to make an annual retreat when I decided to phone Yamada Roshi to ask if I could switch from the practice of *mu* to *kikunushi.* He was very gracious and gave me his approval and an explanation about the practice. I would like to report that this resulted in a great advancement in my *zazen,* but as it turned out I just continued along in the same struggle. Actually it is only in recent years that the heart and value of this practice has been revealed to me.

Although *kikunushi* practice is focused on hearing, it would seem better to broaden the scope of the question so as to search within any concrete action one is engaged in. Who is sitting? Who is breathing? Who is walking? However, we must always remember that these questions are not addressed to the abstracting, categorizing intellect. Their purpose is not to arouse a psychological or philosophical investigation into the nature of one's self. Such a meditation might be interesting, but it would be a precarious path to enlightenment with little probability of success. Some short use of the discursive intellect to *think about* the one who is breathing might be allowed in the beginning to both satisfy and frustrate the monkey mind, but the "Who is breathing?" question is actually addressed to that deep intuitive power by which we know the infinite within the finite, the formless within forms. Earlier in this chapter we called this power the heart or spirit. So this question is used in order to produce a "stirring of the heart." Once this occurs, the words of the question become the vehicle for this stirring as the heart reaches out to advance into the highest level of awareness, i.e. to infinity, to the eternal, unchanging dimension of the self.

The Immanent, Transcendent Self

As an example of some wholesome, reflective intellection that *might* be used to begin this practice, consider the following exercise. Begin by being aware of the pause in your breathing process just before a breath starts. Think to yourself, "A breathing is about to happen." Then during the breathing, "It is now happening." Finally, during the pause at the end, "It is over, ended, gone." Do this three or four times in order to get the feel of your breathing as a *constantly changing* event. To further get the feel for change, close your eyes and imagine the scene outside the place where you are right now. Next visualize the room you are in. Then reflect about what happened to the original image outside. It is gone, superseded by the next image. There has been a change. Finally, reflect that for actual change there must be an enduring subject that does not change as one breath follows another, one image the other. What is this constantly remaining subject like? Here we have returned to our original *kikunushi* question. The one who is hearing, breathing, imagining—what kind of being is it?

In the existential search for the enduring subject underlying all change you must first admit that those breaths, those images were *yours.* You breathed. You visualized. You are in and immanent to all the flow of changes. But at the same time you transcend all the changes. You are there before you start breathing or begin visualizing. You are there after these individual actions are gone. However, the only reality that is both immanent to and transcendent to all changes is the formless. Here we have come to the intellectual pay-off of this exercise. I am formless because I change! To repeat: there can only be true change when there is a changeless subject that underlies all changes. Otherwise there would be nothing but an unconnected series of creation and annihilation and new creations. But there is only "one" changeless. If there were two or more, these would have to have some forms to differentiate them. So you and we and all form beings are ultimately and in essence the changeless, formless one manifesting in a changing universe. To ask "Who is breathing?" leads in the end to infinite potential, to God. The reflective, discursive intellect, however, will never come to the experience of this true self. This is only known by the heart, the spirit. "Who is breathing?" is a spiritual question to be asked whole-heartedly. It will lead us to know our true being and the being of all things.

Finally, we should note that this same basic question can be asked of any action, any event that we witness outside ourselves. When a tree sways in the wind, "What is swaying?" When a flower lifts its face to us, "What is happening here?" The same ultimate answer awaits us. The path of enlightenment is beautifully expressed in the often quoted poem of a Chinese Zen nun.

> Sixty-six times have these eyes beheld the
>   changing seasons.
> Ask me no more of colors and the autumn
>   moon.
> Only listen to the sound of pines and cedars,
>   When no wind stirs.

We can end this still incomplete presentation of mindfulness, the one great spiritual practice, by again bringing to our attention the fundamental Taoist principle of *wu-wei*. Recall that this means "no action for the sake of." It means bare, pure action in itself. Nothing needs to be added to any of our actions (or those of others) for them to reveal the spirit to us. Above all, in mindfulness we give up judgments, comparisons and even thoughts about a purpose or goal. The mind is full of nothing but *what* is happening or *who* is acting. We bring to our perception of each action only bare attention. Each event has its own built-in, existential orientation to stir our hearts and to move us to spirit consciousness. Mind you! This is the fastest, surest way.

15. A Taste of Water

> With joy you will draw water
> from the wells of salvation.
>
> —*Is 12:3*

Frances and Stanley are peacefully walking down a path outside a western city when to their surprise they come across an oriental looking person sitting quietly just by the path in a meditative pose. They are intrigued and mysteriously attracted by the figure, who looks so peaceful and impressive. However, not wanting to disturb the medi- *lu* tation, they start to walk on by. But the person stops them both in their tracks with a melodious "Good morning" and by rising to stand beside them. The whole path seems to somehow brighten at this greeting and by the rising. Fran and Stan are somewhat taken aback and confused, but they cheerily answer, "Good morning."

"May I walk with you?" the figure says. "There is something I would like to share with you."

"Oh, please do. I'm Stanley. Or just Stan."

"And I'm Fran. May I ask your name?"

"My name is Aquarius. I know it sounds a bit strange for a name. It simply means 'water bearer.' And please disregard the masculine ending of this Latin word. I use the form just because it's the one people use for me."

Fran has been wondering whether the person is mascu-line or feminine, so she says, "Oh, then you are a woman?"

"Well, yes. But not only that."

"What do you mean?" asks Stan. "That's pretty con-fusing. Actually I thought you were a man. Aren't you?"

"Yes, I am, Stan. But Fran is right, too."

Fran, who has read a lot of new age literature and is quite open-minded, begins to have a suspicion, so with a touch of both fear and fascination she says, "You sound like you are out of this world. From one of the stars maybe? Where are you from, really? Your clothes seem very oriental."

"Don't worry, Fran. I am very much of this planet and of your age, even though I am, in a way, from the stars. And don't let these clothes fool you. I could just as well be wearing a western suit and tie. It's just that today I want to interact with you more from an eastern viewpoint, so I've adopted an eastern form. But for the moment why don't you take me just as I am and let me share something with you. Are you ready, Stan?"

"This is all pretty strange, but there is something about you that I like and can really trust. What is it that you want to share?"

"Yes, I must say you are intriguing," adds Fran. "What do you want to show us?"

"I'm here to lead you to a taste of water. That is what I am all about. Do you understand?"

Stan thinks deeply for a moment and then answers, "Well, I don't see any drinking faucets around or any spring. Are you talking about water as a symbol of that which you want to share?"

"Very good. Water is one of the best symbols for what I want you to experience."

Fran shakes her head and counters, "But I've heard that there's a beautiful spring down the path from here. I thought you were referring to that. Besides, I'm thirsty."

"Exactly, Fran. Actual water itself is an excellent

'place' to experience reality. Yes, I do want you to taste water from that spring. And I'm so glad that you are thirsty."

"Then we're both right, even though we had different ideas," says Stan.

Aquarius only smiles. "Let's just walk on to the spring. It doesn't cost anything to drink there."[1]

As they walk along both Fran and Stan feel strangely and completely at ease. It's as if they have been walking with Aquarius all their lives. Everything that this amazing being says is new, yet they feel they've known it all along. Their new/old companion smiles broadly as they walk around a bend in the path. Fran's eyes open out wide as she stops in her tracks and cries out, "What a beautiful spring! The water is coming right out of the rock. And so abundantly."

With a vital movement, Stan walks right up to the spring and lets the water splash over his hands. As he does he muses, "It feels so clean and pure. I wonder what it tastes like."

Aquarius smiles even more broadly and says, "Yes I chose this spring because it is so clean. It's nothing but pure water. Taste it."

Both Fran and Stan lean over one by one to drink from the flowing stream. Fran steps back in delight and says, "This is delicious. Just marvelous. But actually it doesn't seem to have any taste at all."

The three sit down on the rocks by the pool at the base of the spring. Aquarius is looking at them. When they both look up and catch this gaze, it is so piercing and powerful that it seems to block out every kind of reflective thought and judgment. Stan blurts out almost without thinking,

"Yes, it really doesn't have any taste at all. And this is what you want us to taste."

Aquarius only smiles and looks down at the water in the pool.

"It doesn't have any color either, does it?" says Fran. "But when you see anything in the water, it's color becomes so much more visible and true."

Aquarius looks at her again, beaming, while Stan continues to muse with wonder in his voice, "You know, it doesn't have any shape either. It's formless. It always has a shape, but that's completely determined by whatever it's in."

Even as he says this Stan doesn't know where his thought comes from. Aquarius nods and laughs delightedly, and then, turning to them both, says, "Stan, Fran, look into the pool of water. What do you see?"

Fran becomes a child again. Although she has seen the phenomenon a thousand times before, she exclaims, "I see my face. How amazing! I never realized . . ."

Stan is equally amazed. "Yea, I see me. But I also see you, Fran, and Aquarius and everything around us. I never realized . . ."

Aquarius looks at both of them sharply. "What didn't you realize?"

"Well," Fran stammers, "somehow it's not just a reflection. I am the water. I mean . . ."

"Do you mean that you are *this* water?" interrupts Aquarius.

"Yes. It sounds crazy, but . . . This water is, of course, this water. And I am I. But I am flowing out of the rock and in the pool."

"That's what I mean, too," echoes Stan. "And somehow I am you and Fran and everything."

Aquarius' gaze is gentler now, and loving, yet still inquiring. "But you both agree that water is without any taste or color or shape at all. Are you like that?")

"Yes," says Fran excitedly.

"And no!" nods Stan laughing.

"Now who's being confusing?" retorts the delighted Aquarius.

"It's not confusing at all," cries Fran. "Just mysterious."

"Yes," answers Stan. "And totally commonplace."

They walk as one along the path beside the waters flowing from the spring. Fran and Stan can't take their eyes off the stream. It has revealed so much to them and seems to hold promise of more and more reality, even though what they have already seen is boundless. Finally Aquarius stops them and points down into the flowing stream. They both kneel down and peer closely at the clear water. Again their usual thinking and reflection is dissipated. They are not gazing _at_ the water but _into_ it, into themselves.

Fran says softly not to herself but about herself, "Water."

They hear Aquarius murmur, "With joy you will draw water from the springs of salvation." Again there is an added murmur, "Form, this is the formless. Formless, this is form."

As the two continue to look into the water/self, the tiny stream expands to cosmic dimensions. Their experience advances to find themselves and everything as only one great flowing stream. Then with no sense of interruption or interference they hear Aquarius change the symbolism, "Relax. Rejoice and play in the one breath of heaven and earth." And shortly after, "There is only the dance, only the dance."

With one accord the two stand up to continue along the path with their companion. Everything they see now

glows with energy and infinite radiance. Anything and everything seems within their power. Fran dances lightly
along, intoning, "I'm alive. I'm alive. This is what it is to
be alive."

At this some words from the gospel come into Stan's
mind, "The water I shall give them will become in them a
spring of water welling up to eternal life." He looks at
Aquarius, who only smiles and nods. Stan looks at their
companion master intently and says, "I know who you are.
You are a Christ. You are the Christ consciousness. You
are what we are programmed to be. That's why this stream
is actually a river of living water flowing from within us."

They walk in silence for a while, basking in the wonder
of their very being. Fran is thinking, "Now I know why we
are baptized in water and how water turns into wine and
gladdens human hearts." Finally a question begins to arise
in her mind and, although she somehow knows the answer
already, she seems to need its articulation. "How did we
come to this state of awareness and how can we preserve it
and grow?"

Aquarius lifts up the arms of his eastern robe and
almost chants:

> Let your mind wander in simplicity,
> blend your spirit with vastness,
> follow along with things the way they are,
> and make no room for egoistic views.

Then finally, as the path turned back toward the city
and their ordinary lives, Aquarius urges them, "Remember
that water follows the line of least resistance. Let go. Let
flow. Let go of comparisons, judgments, fears and con-

frontations. Entrust yourself to your Self. I am your Self. It's all very simple."

"And it's all right *here!*" says Stan.

"And *now!*" cries Fran.

They all continue walking along the path together, happy to share a taste of water.

see p 108
2'in the Beatitude

APPENDIX A

A QUESTIONNAIRE:
TOWARD THE DISCOVERY
OF ONE'S SPIRITUAL PATH

Directions: 1. Answer the questions spontaneously without too much reflection.
2. Ignore the letters in parentheses after some of the items.

1. What names or titles of Jesus of Nazareth do you most prefer? Choose at least two, and not more than five.

A.	Priest	(D, a, k)	Q.	Life	(a, K)
B.	Master	(D, a, k)	R.	Hero	(D)
C.	Friend	(D, a, k)	S.	Bread of Life	(K)
D.	Beloved	(D)	T.	Redeemer	(D, A)
E.	Lord	(D, a, k)	U.	Son of God	(D, K)
F.	Good Shepherd	(D)	V.	Healer	(D, a, k)
G.	Teacher	(K)	W.	Sacred Heart	(D)
H.	Alpha & Omega	(K)	X.	Emmanuel	(D, K)
I.	King (of Kings)	(D, a)	Y.	Savior	(D, A, K)
J.	Light of the World	(K)	Z.	Way	(a, K)
K.	Brother	(D)	Aa.	Prince of Peace	(D, A, K)
L.	Suffering Servant	(D)	Bb.	Truth	(K)
M.	Christ (Messiah)	(K)	Cc.	Leader	(D, a)
N.	Son of Man	(L)	Dd.	Revolutionary	(A)
O.	Cosmic Christ	(K)	Ee.	Lamb of God	(D)
P.	Victim	(D)	Ff.	(other) _____	

2. Other than Jesus and Mary, name three saints or other great persons that you feel an affinity with and wish to imitate.

A. _____ B. _____ C. _____

3. Other than the Bible, name three or four of your favorite books.

A. _____ B. _____
C. _____ D. _____

216

4. How would you characterize your attitude toward work? Check as many as you wish.
For me, work is:

A. _____ my duty (K, a)
B. _____ my prayer (A)
C. _____ my service for the Lord (D, a)
D. _____ spreading God's love (D)
E. _____ play, my enjoyment (A)
F. _____ self-sacrifice for the Lord (D)
G. _____ my service for others (D)
H. _____ a path to enlightenment (K)
I. _____ my contentment (A)
J. _____ way to experience reality (K)
K. _____ giving witness to the gospel (D, a)
L. _____ place to discover the meaning of life (K)

5. Do you use images and imagination in prayer?
Choose one: Never or only sometimes _____ (D, k)
Often or very often _____ (D)

6. Do you prefer to simply *be* at prayer?
Choose one: Yes _____ (A)
Not really _____ (K, D)

7. Do you think quite a lot when you pray (not including distractions)?
Choose one: No or not much _____ (A, d)
Quite a bit or very much _____ (K, d)

8. What is your favorite form of prayer? _____

9. When you fail in doing something, which of the following would you most instinctively say:

A. "Oh, I'm sorry!" (D)   B. "Oh, how stupid!" (K)
C. "Oh, what can I do about this?" (A)

10. When are you most bored?

A. When there's nothing but small talk going on. (K)

B. When there's nobody to talk to and to have fun with.   (D)
C. When there's nothing to do.   (A)

11. How would you characterize yourself?

As a:

A.	Student	(K)	I.	Artisan	(A)
B.	Poet	(K, D)	J.	Executive	(A)
C.	Administrator	(A)	K.	Servant	(D, A)
D.	Devotee	(D)	L.	Teacher	(K)
E.	Questioner	(K)	M.	Doer	(A)
F.	Artist	(A, K)	N.	Philosopher	(K)
G.	Lover	(D)	O.	Fan	(D)
H.	Intellectual	(K)	P.	Thinker	(K)
			Q.	(other) _____	

12. When you are at work, what are your habitual points of attention.

A. efficiency   (A)
B. that others will think well of you   (D, K)
C. that others will think well of your work   (A, K)
D. to show your love for Jesus Christ or God   (D)
E. that the work accomplishes its purpose   (A, K)
F. to please superior(s)   (D, K)
G. to imitate someone else   (D)
H. to show love for others   (D)
I. to find a sense of one's flow of life   (K)
J. to gain or maintain membership in a group (community)   (D)
K. your own standard of neatness   (A, K)
L. just the work with little attention to anything else   (A)
M. to do God's will   (D)
N. to avoid the displeasure of your superior(s)   (K)
O. to sense the very purpose of life   (A, K)

APPENDIX B

To interpret your questionnaire, first read the section on the three paths carefully (Chapter 8). Using the norms given there consider each of your answers. Into which orientation (path) does this answer seem to put me? Note that some of the answers could pertain to not just one but two or even three paths. However, the simple multiplicity of items should bring out your characteristic orientation. The letters in parentheses after many answers indicate the paths these items would usually pertain to. "D"–devotion; "A"–action; "K"–knowledge. Lower case letters (a, d, k) indicate that this item refers more to the path indicated by the capital letter(s) than to this (these).

To concretely interpret your questionnaire first analyze your answers to those questions which do not have letters in parentheses.

2. Ask yourself what it is you most admire about the saints you have chosen—their devotion or active or knowledge characteristics? For example, do you admire Francis of Assisi for his great devotion to Jesus and to the Father (D) or for his intimacy with creatures (D, k) or for his service of the poor (A, d), etc.? In this way you can put letters to each of your answers.

3. In the same way as in 2, ask yourself what it is that attracts you in these books and how each book has affected you. Does it move you to action, to devotion to God and others, or does it delight you with its intuitions? Again, assign letters to each of your answers.

8. It is up to you to determine into which category/ies your prayer form best fits. For example, the rosary would usually be devotional, but you might see that you are using it like a mantra with little or no thought and with no object to whom you are praying. In such a case it would be

the prayer of a K person with perhaps some element of A as well.

When you have diagnostic letters for all your answers, total up all the letters in each category using separate totals for lower and upper case letters. Already the basic orientation/s of your path should be apparent. However, if you wish to refine the totals further, you can assign 2 points to each upper case letter and 1 point to each lower case and thus arrive at point totals. As to those answers that have 2 or 3 upper case letters, it will be up to your own judgment to choose one letter and omit the other/s or to reduce it/them to lower case.

Please note that this questionnaire is still in a developmental stage. It is included here because, even as it is, it has helped many along their paths.

NOTES

Preface

1. *Sunday Examiner,* Catholic Diocese Center, Hong Kong, February 12, 1988.
2. Swami Abhishiktananda, *Hindu Christian Meeting Point, Within the Cave of the Heart,* trans. Sara Grant, RSCJ (Bombay: Institute of Indian Culture, 1969) p. 107.
3. Ibid. p. 109.

Chapter 1

1. This and all the poems of Silesius quoted in this book are from F. Franck, trans., *The Book of Angelus Silesius* (New York: Random House, 1976).
2. All translations from *Tao Te Ching* are our own.

Chapter 2

1. This and the two accounts below are all taken from *Kyosho,* Sambo Koryukai, Shunjusha Press, Tokyo. We have substituted initials for names to preserve the anonymity often preferred in such accounts.

Chapter 3

1. Quoted in *Toward a Philosophy of Zen Buddhism* by T. Izutsu (Boulder, Col.: Prajna Press, 1982) p. 208.

Chapter 4

1. C. Potok, *Book of Lights* (New York: Alfred A. Knopf, 1981) p. 292.
2. Quoted in *From Glory to Glory,* Gregory of Nyssa's Mysti-

cal Writings, trans. H. Musurillo, S.J. (New York: Charles Scribner's Sons, 1981) p. 126.

3. Evagrius Ponticus, *The Praktikos & Chapters On Prayer,* trans. J.E. Bamberger, OCSO (Kalamazoo: Cistercian Publications, 1981) (#4) p. 56, (#11) p. 57, (#117) p. 75.

4. M. Fox, *Original Blessing* (Santa Fe: Bear and Co., 1983) p. 137.

5. Ibid.

6. Ibid.

7. Quoted in *The Teaching of the Mystics* by Walter Stace (New York: New American Library, 1960) p. 155.

8. W. Capps and W. Wright, *Silent Fire* (San Francisco: Harper and Row, 1978) p. 155.

9. Quoted in *Newsweek,* December 31, 1984, p. 63.

10. Fox, op. cit. p. 88.

Chapter 5

1. R.P. McBrien, *Catholicism,* Vol. I (Minneapolis: Winston Press, 1970) p. 333.

Chapter 6

1. Joan Metzner, M.M., *Seasons of Life* (Maryknoll: Maryknoll Sisters of St. Dominic, Inc., 1981) p. 7.

2. Ken Wilber, *Up From Eden* (Boulder, Col.: Shambala, 1983).

3. Quoted in Wilber, p. 317.

4. Ibid. pp. 316–317.

5. Ibid. p. 317.

6. Ibid. pp. 317–318.

Chapter 7

1. W. Kasper, *Jesus the Christ* (New York: Paulist Press, 1976) p. 114.

2. John Cobb, *Beyond Dialogue: Toward a Mutual Transfor-*

mation of Christianity and Buddhism (Philadelphia: Fortress Press, 1982) p. 90.

3. Quoted in W. Stace, ibid. p. 156.

4. Ken Wilber, *Eye to Eye: The Quest for the New Paradigm* (New York: Doubleday, 1983) p. 88.

5. Quoted in Wilber, *Up From Eden,* p. 248.

Chapter 9

1. Quoted in W. Stace, ibid., pp. 24–25.

2. P. Kapleau, *The Three Pillars of Zen* (Boston: Beacon Press, 1967) p. 205.

Chapter 10

1. All the quotations from Chuang Tzu in this chapter are taken from B. Watson's translation, Columbia University Press, 1918.

Chapter 13

1. Fox, ibid., p. 67.

Chapter 14

1. Quoted in *Essays in Zen Buddhism,* First Series, by D.T. Suzuki (York Beach, Maine: Samuel Weiser, Inc., 1985) pp. 200–201.

Chapter 15

1. As our readers will recognize, we have woven into this fantasy a number of biblical and other texts. We list them here in order of appearance.
   a. Isaiah 55:1 (Drink without cost)
   b. Numbers 20:11 (Water from the rock)
   c. Matthew 18:3 (Unless you become like little children)
   d. Isaiah 12:3 (Draw water with joy)

e. Heart Sutra (Form is the formless)
f. Chuang Tzu, Chapter 6 (The one breath of heaven and earth)
g. T.S. Eliot, *Burnt Norton* (Only the dance)
h. John 4:14 (A spring welling up to eternal life)
i. John 7:38 (A river from within)
j. John 2:1ff and Psalm 104:15 (Wine that gladdens)
k. Chuang Tzu, Chapter 7 (Let your mind wander . . .)

166° experience centered reading of Bibb. (Philip)

180 (det 4:12

for - alive light, strong, able.

202 ha hum - "Have an quiet time"

abundant Lf

2/4 "what we are programmed to be" - as Lf was ordered

radical
ill
we

133 4-5 f "Y life goal "To be a free, easy wanderer" "of Jesus" lifestyle open to
a free, spontaneous, natural, joyful way of life. Heaven
life in the Spirit (4 Paul) 145 quote
called "Life at the Summit"

143 "Is this the real world ?? No — it's the evil ones right

& Ch 10 Life in the Spirit — 145 quote

148 "The Chr goal "To enter into the X-st experience

153 The Yin-Yang symbol explained

156 why goddess! Because babies (life) comes fr mother
157 & Biblical "Lord" is male + power

169 a good def. of repentance = radical shift ...

171 esoteric = "inner" as exoteric = "outer"

174 Mk & Grow in "the Pure Land"

175 on Shalom: nothing is lacking, have come to infinite
                                              completion
172f   175 The Beatitudes thru Oriental eyes   (4 Paul)

177 John "Sign" defined X

— 178f Jn 2 read allegorically, or esoterically — "best wine" nos. 180

*182 The "Law" is not something imposed outward but the law of your
            being, Isah 10, Jer 31, etc
                                                      bottom
184 In Zen dai go tettei = great enlightenment piercing to the
                          to the very source of   being
v 185 "baptism" plunging one's whole being into the Spirit
            movement (Rom 6-7 etc)

187 Weil: "The universe is a conspiracy organized for my benefit"
                    (how 2 win)
* 190 In East doing precedes understanding, vice-versa in
                    (Jn 7 "know if you do" etc)   West
            "we go in mind first" X

196 "Bodies are temples of Spirit" x f Cor

Phil 2 v 202 "Lose your mind! come to your senses" y
                                      (Anthony de Mello)

v 203 Old Latin saying "Do you what are doing"

203 "2; the flowers became one!

Lorna Baer wk. 332-4020

(Joyce Dano daughter)

- "Cognitive map" psy. say - a organizd way to Church

X 109 heart - "The sp. energy center"
199 "able to see w/ the clarity of dawn"
                        dawn". Jn 9 ch

X A descrip^g no. 110 : 108-9
   (told to Dr. Jordan)

113 mecanismo! "the virginite in manifestation"
   semon

93 evolutionic "agei (past
   eternal "ageo" (future)
138 "the ego mind"

48 "God: naked being"

68 Th Kat's question - can an
limitless - infinite God be incarnate in
   man -- mans is one?

91-² Phil 2 - Kenosis
   (89 C)
99 I Sew 1: 3+ 14 we became god.
103 Hab 3 - " "

        [signature]

Heb 2 "perceie" - we let fallow for we God?
   1 u 99

45 Ex 3: 14 "2 am "
   "Jahweh' is 3ᵈ person of text
   1e "He who is"
   but not attribute - God is Love
                        etc

47 14 9 II 12. (Pauli
   41   experience

69 ° Gen 3 X the trad
   veto well stated, but
   questionable
   An upward fall? 74?

Ch 6 - 9 Eastern
   rewriting of
   Gen 3 -- sort of
   gnostic

102 up 14 "you shine as light"
   Phil
151 14 term for "all they need
   heir" M !, Heb 1:1-2;
                        3 !

165 14 M +5 "pure of heart"
168 "transvaluation of values"
X 170 Makapoi = the blessedness
   of the gods
v 172 Jap. version "Blessed
   are those who know their
   own poverty"

177 "reign" is John defined X

182 14 acts 2 literalized

191 14 Jesus "as a man
   of all Phil"